Leaving

Your

Light On

Inspirational Stories of Unforgettable Lives

Dear Kevin & Christie,

Thank you for your trust & kindness
to allow me to share my passion.

KELLY A. MELOCHE

Love,

Kelly

For more information or to book an event contact:
kelly@kellymeloche.com
or visit: *www.kellymeloche.com*

ISBN: 978-1-959555-77-3 (Print)

The Platypus Team
Platypus Publishing
support@mattrud.com

DEDICATION

I dedicate this book to Jaime & Kara. Without both of you, I would never have known the pure joy of a Momma Bear's love.

ACKNOWLEDGEMENT

This book is the gift of the beautiful people that championed me to its completion. Thank you for your immeasurable love.

I, also, can never adequately express my gratitude to the families that have welcomed me into their sacred circle of trust, while at their most depleted moments. It is a true honour to be able to share the beautiful stories of lives well-lived.

I am a better human for having the privilege to share in the experience of celebrating lives in such a deserving way.

REFLECTIONS

A funeral is not for the dead, it is for the living. Kelly has a unique ability to craft the life of your loved one into an awesome celebration of a life uniquely lived. People leave Kelly's services saying that was a "good funeral." As a funeral director, those are the best words to hear. You know the family is leaving a very sad event with a full heart.

~Kevin Reid, President, Reid Funeral home

In more than 3 decades of working in hospitals and hospices with the dying and their families, I can attest to the immeasurable value of the profound healing that happens when families create memorable farewells. "Leaving your Light On" is a must read for everyone, especially those who work with the dying and their families or those who are currently living the reality.

~Maria Giannotti MA, MSc,
Specialist in End of Life Care and Spirituality

Kelly is the best and most versatile celebrant I know. It takes a lot of energy to obtain life stories from family members. Then, in a short period of time, Kelly articulates those memories into a meaningful celebration of life. This is a true talent. Kelly goes above and beyond with every family she serves; sharing these stories is a gift.

~Brian Parent,
Managing Director/Founder, Families First

Kelly is a magical storyteller. Her gift is being able to bring a persons life back to their family in a way that is truly inspirational. Everyone leaving a funeral that was led by Kelly always says, "I want my funeral to feel just like that."

~Lorna Baker, Managing Funeral Director

TABLE OF CONTENTS

FORWARD

I am the storyteller of lives well-lived; lives that were epic in love, and lives muddled by darkness. Lives that inspired either through brilliance or brokenness. Every life is important, and every life ends with a story rich in lessons and rewards to ripple us into safety and sanity if we listen.

The first time I felt the kaleidoscope of bewildering emotions was at my neighbour's funeral. I was 12, and my favourite babysitter had been killed in a car accident. I was baffled how hard everyone tried to not act sad, angry, or confused. And nobody wanted to talk about Joanne, who was just about the coolest person I knew. After that day, it seemed wrong to talk about her. Death, I wondered, was maybe the time that you were supposed to erase the person from your being. Clear the cache of love, memories and lessons. At least that is how everyone acted.

Two weeks after my 20th birthday, my father died. Seven years later, my mom followed. I have zero recollection of their funerals, aside from feeling as if it were a survival mission to remain numb, say the right things, and to hover above the dark abyss as if it wasn't happening. Their funerals, just like Joanne's, had nothing to do with the lives that they lived. Hence, they mostly remain a mystery to me. I don't know their stories aside from the fragments I remember. Their services were an assortment of rhetoric, canned language and bookmarked psalms delivered by someone who didn't give a shit about the person we loved and the untold story they lived to the best of their human ability.

No wonder everyone hates going to a funeral! When a baby is born, we gather to celebrate. We talk about their life, what we hope for them, the happiness they deserve and their birthright to give and receive great love. We validate their life. When the circle closes, and it will for every single one of us, shouldn't the story we lived then be shared as a final act to let our light settle into those who will be moving on as the torch carriers of our legacy?

Of course it should.

This book is a selection of the life stories I have had the privilege to write and deliver after these humble warriors, gentle misunderstood wanderers and a few pains in the asses earned their wings.

It is meant to remind you of your own story. It will one day be told. Maybe by me!

What would your title be?

PRELUDE

If you are old enough to remember the 1960's CBS show, "The Munsters," then you'd understand when I tell you I grew up feeling as though I was the kindred spirit to Marilyn. I was the youngest of 2, until, of course, I found out there were more—all sisters, never the brother I desperately yearned for. That was just one more little kernel hidden in the tickle trunk of family secrets. Daily living was, from my observation, a poker game of illusions. I continually wondered who was the alien... them or me?

I was learning that I loved a good story, and was to discover that mine was to be found when I stepped out of unnecessary haze and into a labyrinth of unfolding clarity.

My memories circle back to the early years when independence was the key to peace. After selecting, literally, the most mismatched clothing ensemble and crunching back half a sugar-soaked grapefruit that had hardened overnight in the fridge, I was off to slay grade 2.

Once out the door, I was on a quest to make my way through my "Pleasantville" neighbourhood seeking healthy glimmers of family values, good sense, and snippets of stories in the making. I had two stops along the way. Both were olive branches of hope. The first stop was the Gilberts. Two parents and 5 kids whose bellies were filled with warm oatmeal and family intention. Same with the next stop. Those friends met us at the park, a drop off from Dad every day. I loved how my friends, Amy and Samantha, would joke about all the things that mattered that morning. They knew and understood their roots.

I was the smiling actress along the way, hoping my straight A's and untamed curls would somehow mask how deeply unacquainted I was with myself.

This became a trend. While always trying to flesh out my truths and genuine purpose, I gained insight by witnessing the journeys of others. I cared. My Mom used to call me "Little Ann Landers" because it seemed my ears attracted stories and my shoulders were for tears. Other people made sense to me. I liked connecting their dots while learning immensely from their lives.

I didn't know it, but I was in a lifelong boot camp preparing for a career that I had no idea existed.

As a little girl, I'd sit on my bed and pretend to read stories to my invisible audience. I just loved that feeling of engagement. I adored dipping my essence into the story and embodying the journey as if it were my own. Whether it was a fairy tale or fiction, I was always a willing passenger, jumping aboard to be moved through the landscape of their lessons.

Once I became an adult, every career I excelled at meant that I was communicating with others more than effectively. In my early twenties I went into law enforcement. I have no idea why, really. If I am honest, I think my mother nudged me that way, and I was too eager to please. We've all bought that t-shirt or a similar one, right? Had I not drunk too much of that people pleasing Kool-Aid, I very well might have taken my straight A's to medical school and achieved my dream of making house calls with my retro doctor's bag. Which, I guess, would have pleased people too, but I would have arrived by virtue of my own nudging.

Standing a mere five feet tall and wearing a smile that never dims seemed to totally contradict the handcuffs strapped to my duty belt. I wore a badge from age 20 until I couldn't silence my entrepreneurial spirit another second, throwing myself into the "if you can dream, you can be it" world. I opened up what would become a grassroots global healthcare company by age 40. It made absolutely zero sense, if I am to be realistic. I was a single mother by this time, with two kids in grade school who were enrolled in all the expensive sports. All I can say is that faith kicked my fear's ass every single day when I felt myself seeking sanity as I sorted socks.

The next 13 years were filled with extensive travel, meeting incredible thought leaders and embracing inspiration. I battled with feeling worthy and sometimes felt I didn't believe in myself to even a fraction of what it appeared others did. The "imposter syndrome" is what they call it, and I had a hefty dose.

One time I was at a luncheon for "Women Entrepreneurial World Leaders" at Caesar's Palace in Las Vegas. There, at one of the beautifully set tables for 8, was my name tag. Close as I could tell, they did their research and concluded that I was worth the buffet. There was a panel of women that had paid oodles of money in order to commandeer the mic for a measured period of time. They all deserved every second, especially Miss Turkey, as I nicknamed her. While I don't remember the details of her presentation, which I have no doubt were riveting, it was the few moments in which she finessed from performer to mother that woke me up. During her presentation she not-so-apologetically took a phone call. Turns out it was her daughter's 5th birthday and, in that moment, Miss Turkey won the crown as far as I was concerned. When she returned back to the moment at hand, she remarked that all we have, every day, is really just ourselves. It is the person looking back in the mirror that counts and is accountable. Miss Turkey owned her authentic ground, stepped outside of the pinstriped business casual norm, staying true to the woman in her mirror and her tiny treasure halfway around the world.

A God-smacked moment, gifted to me from a stranger, that I have since adored.

The next day was my turn. I was the Keynote speaker! Kelly Meloche—lit up in lights. The woman in my mirror was a jittery mess! The room went from sparsely populated to standing room only. The power point presentation queued up belonged to a presenter from Afghanistan, so when the timer went off, all I had was me! What a gloriously, somewhat paralyzing, gifted mistake turned opportunity.

I was too short for the podium, and there was no deflecting attention to my presentation on the screen once it was properly loaded, so I stood in front of the crowd, a very humbled and grateful woman with something to share. I knew my research well enough that doing that "talk to the screen" defense mechanism would have been such a massive waste of the moment I was blessed with. I didn't talk to, I engaged with, the strangers and their variety of eye colours and expressions. I believed in my craft, and that became the energy of the room.

Three more similar sessions followed, all of which went outrageously different than what I had practiced to my same lifelong invisible groupies. My notes became relatively secondary. They were a means to guide but not lead. Subconsciously, I had stopped believing in the assumed divide between myself and the people offering me their time and attention. It was about being collectively receptive to the room, a gathering of good intentions and aspiring ambitions. They were a lovely lot of humans, some of which I am now privileged to call friend.

My life was unfolding much to the tune of John Lennon's, "Life is what happens as you're busy making plans." While I thought I was becoming a rescue squad to the waitlists plaguing Canada's socialized medical system, I was just being distracted. Evolution comes in many forms. This was part of my spiritual journey, leading me to cast deeper roots into a level of care that all this globe-trotting was preparing me for. Soon I realized…

Boot camp was over!

I sold my company, opened my mind as wide as my ambitions could see as I coaxed purpose, once again, to marry with my passion.

A proverbial blink occurred, then a refreshingly charismatic man from the funeral home business asked to meet with me. Let's be real, when have you ever heard 'charismatic' and 'funeral' being used in the same sentence? Initially, he was hopeful that I could help him in his quest to transform his funeral homes from gloomy to gracious. I held little hope. As I looked around while listening to his wishes, it felt paradoxical. There was no evidence of overt momentum to modernization.

We shared great synergy. I immediately gravitated to his crisp, creative intelligence, but I couldn't see the end game. It was evident we were supposed to meet but were unsure of the reason why. As our chats gained momentum, he finally exclaimed, "Kelly, you are a born Celebrant."

I had no idea what that meant.

It meant I would listen to people. It meant I would write the life stories of their loved ones. It meant I would tell these stories to people who aren't invisible... okay, yes, some are, but they are the guest of honour!

As they delve into the past and recount stories, families and friends uncover a wealth of discoveries. The conversations flow naturally, unveiling beautiful gems of cherished moments that signify the start of their path to healing.

All of their favourite things are included in this celebration. The Harley Davidson and a sea of biker colours with a ride at the end to roar farewell. A shot of whisky, nip of Merlot, perhaps the artwork that told its own stories, best friends who can barely squeak out a song from their past as love wells up in the back of their throats, favourite pets, awards and the music that feels like a B12 shot right to your soul.

Life is a magnificent trail of stories. Not one is perfect, but they are all filled with inspiration, and even in the tragedy, we find love.

Everyday people are extraordinary people! When I tell their story, whether it is at a funeral home, in a backyard, on a boat and yes, even near a goat, it is what peace and comfort are all about.

Celebrating a life after it is fully lived is essential, it is respectful, and it really does put the "fun" in funeral!

CHAPTER ONE

JOHN AND KATHARINA GRUNDNER

Because Love Never Dies

During World War II, Russian soldiers invaded and pillaged the village of Kurd in Hungary. In 1944, the soldiers returned and, with the help of the mayor, took away only those of German heritage between the ages of 18 to 36.

Katharina, an 18-year-old of German heritage, was taken without warning and had only 15 minutes to get ready. Her mother was devastated upon returning to find her child gone and feared the worst.

After being taken from their village in Hungary, Katharina and others of German heritage were loaded onto trucks, then into the cattle cars of a train and transported to Kadiivka, a town in Ukraine. Some did not survive the journey, and the Russian soldiers disposed of their bodies every three days.

Upon arrival, they were forced to sleep in a barn without amenities and given very little to eat or drink, causing starvation. They worked on a farm every day except Sundays, initially on a vegetable farm and then in apple and pear orchards. They began the practice of hiding and eating the small amount of food they were given until a sympathetic Russian soldier allowed them to eat some fruit when no one else was around.

The prisoners were moved to army barracks for their third year of captivity, where they had to sleep on boards with straw and walk four kilometers to work in the coal mines with no amenities. After work, they had to take communal showers and sleep in the same clothes they worked in. A Russian security guard allowed them to sneak coal to neighbouring homes in exchange for cabbage soup. The emptied and hopeless prisoners feared they may never see their loved ones again and believed this was how their lives would end. Katharina held tight to her prayers of a life that would become gentle, kind and comforting.

In 1947, Katharina and 72 others were sent back to Hungary from Kurd by the Russians to make room for captured German soldiers. Only 34 survived the journey, with some dying from freezing or starvation.

Katharina was part of a group consisting of six women and one man. The man, a cousin of her mother, had also been in Ukraine. They felt safer in his presence and stayed close to each other for protection.

Upon returning to Hungary, they found all Hungarians of German ancestry had been evicted from Hungary. The group managed to travel from Hungary back to Germany using cigarettes and paprika as currency. They arrived in Rosenthal, Germany on Dec. 13, 1947, which was also Katharina's mother's birthday.

It would be just one short and recuperative year before Katharina's enchanting story would commence. While her journey had been an arduous one, she was starting to feel the sparkles of her future arrive. Her biggest clue was John, a handsome young man that she met in Hungary. Their paths intersected once again in Germany. John danced his way right into Katharina's heart as their two souls united as one.

As Paulo Coelho said, "If you're brave enough to say goodbye, life will reward you with a new hello."

Oct. 1, 1948 marked the day when Katharina and John exchanged their marriage vows at the Town Hall. Following German tradition, they also celebrated a Catholic wedding ceremony, the very next day, on Oct. 2. With the arrival of their two daughters, Heidi and Martha, their love grew stronger, and they aspired for a better life for their family.

In 1953, they embarked on a journey across the Atlantic, accompanied by their daughters and John's mother, Anna. Their new home, Canada, welcomed them with open arms in Montreal, Quebec, or as the locals say, "bienvenue."

Life was about to become softer, even though work, hard

work, would remain a way of life. They made their home in Kingsville, Ontario, residing in the top of a house and working mainly in the tobacco fields. Katharina soon discovered that while cleaning houses, if someone asked if she was hungry, it was a query about her tummy, not her nationality. This led to a comical misunderstanding where lunch always seemed to appear out of nowhere.

By 1956, the family, now including a son, Herb, relocated to Leamington. Katharina donned her invisible cape and embodied the role of a super mom with incredible grace. She worked all three shifts at Heinz, sold Avon products, attended English classes at the high school and effortlessly whipped up traditional dishes such as schnitzel, goulash and Swiss steak. She topped off each meal with a delectable homemade dessert, never breaking a sweat and always sharing her smile.

During the 1990s, Katharina became a well-known figure at Curves, where she rocked her own style of a "diva." Her infectious laughter was a trademark that was recognized by everyone who knew her.

Meanwhile, John reveled in a sense of loyalty to his new country and accepted his Canadian citizenship with great pride. He never lost sight of his gratitude to share the soil, butcher the English language and always find a hill to send his kids down on a toboggan, soaking in every morsel of their laughter and squeals.

On a brisk November day, Katharina exhaled one last time

after sharing her glorious spirit with the world for 96 deserving years.

Together, she and her John blessed the world for 74 inspirational years.

As John sat at Katharina's Celebration of Life, he was 99 years young. Specialists indicated he was dealing with a diagnosis of advanced Alzheimer's disease. Grace filled the room and Alzheimer's was nowhere to be seen when it came to John on that day. He was, without a doubt, fully present in the moment, soaking in the love and every word spoken.

As it was time to say the final goodbye, John began to lift himself out of his wheelchair, determined to walk towards his best friend and treasured love. With conviction, he declared, "I am a man."

Fifty-five days later, John answered Katharina's whispers and joined her in the next phase of their soul commitment. We can only imagine the exaltation of the heavens as John peacefully floated into Katharina's waiting arms. In gratitude, we smile for their reunion.

Because love never dies…only people do.

> *"What greater thing is there for two human souls than to feel that they are joined to strengthen each other and to be one with each other in silent unspeakable memories."*
> *~ George Eliot*

CHAPTER TWO

LEONARDO SANTAMARIA

The Ten Year Old Barber

We recognize an era to be a long and distinct period of history with a particular feature or characteristic. My heart sings with the recognition of an era that was truly magnificent, marked by the shining presence of Leonardo Santamaria! His journey spanning 86 years, 10 months and 29 days marks period of time when the world shone brighter by pure virtue of Leonardo's presence.

Leonardo was the smiling, gregarious, zinfandel-pushing icon of South Windsor, who effortlessly exhaled altruism throughout each chapter of his life that made his era, one that will be never forgotten, and always treasured.

His accent was as memorable as his infectious laughter when he attempted to navigate the complexities of the English language. Oh, how we long to hear Leonardo report the fog one more time, with his classic expression of "such a fucky day."

Leonardo's unique perspective and infectious personality lit up the world around him. His irreverent humour was a source of endless delight. Even in the midst of the most mundane days, he had a way of bringing a smile to everyone's face and lifting countless spirits.

The era of Leonardo Santamaria began in Monte Sant' Angelo, Italy. Upon his arrival, he was given a name that rolls off your tongue like poetry and most likely left his parents breathless. Leonardo came from meagre, actually less than meagre, beginnings. It was a humble start to a remarkable journey. He was raised in an environment where your riches were faith, and thriving became evident by your ability to always remain hopeful that the best is yet to come.

At the age of 10, Leonardo set out make a contribution to his world by becoming a barber. Yes, you read that right, a 10-year-old barber! This was the moment when he stepped into his divine purpose. Leonardo was a natural giver, and the more he gave, the more expansive his life experience became. Cutting hair and giving a smooth shave were his gateways into the hearts of countless people. This was only the beginning to a greatness of epic proportions.

Leonardo's father was going back and forth from Italy to Canada at the time to work at CN Rail. Leonardo and his siblings were offered Canadian status if they wanted it, but they had to act quickly.

At 17 years old, Leonardo and his 19-year-old brother left every comfort and love that they had ever known, packed up their faith and a few other belongings for Canada. Little did Leonardo know what a game changer, a rescuer of countless underdogs, and a Picasso of Personality he was put on this earth to be.

Without a word of English in his linguistic arsenal, Leonardo shone his bright smile as he settled into the City of Roses, Windsor, Ontario, doing as much as he could to find his way. If he was asked how he was doing at the time, he would have likely responded with, "I am good, but I lie."

In 1952, just 18 years young and armed with the audacity and courage of youth, Leonardo walked into a barbershop on Wyandotte St. to apply for a job indicating he had eight years of experience. If you wanted to count the two years he spent selling cigarettes or bartering for bread on the black market with the US soldiers who took over his small town in Italy, well then, he had 10 years of work experience. Perhaps we could call that his Public Relations skillset? Of course, the Barber interviewing him must have thought Leo was a bit questionable, especially since most of his answers were "yes & no" but he trusted his intuition and allowed Leo to show him his talent. This marked Leonardo's first job and a magnificent turning point in his life.

Each day as young Leonardo worked his magic with scissors and clippers, he also honed his stalking prowess. Beatrice was a young hair stylist that worked in the same building. She wasn't aware of it at first but her magnetic pull to Leonardo was changing his currents and shaping his stars.

Leonardo began some covert operations on his own. When he learned where Beatrice caught the bus, he'd mutter to himself, "Oh, thanks God." Then, of course, oh so casually, he'd board the same bus which took him to nowhere close to where he lived… just to spend time acting like he wasn't trying to spend time with the girl that he loved for all the right reasons.

Finally, Leonardo enhanced his courting rituals to actual conversations which led to Beatrice bringing what his family thought was some "way too smooth Casanova" home. He was met by what he referred to as, "the crew." Likeable Leonardo was in a pickle! It got worse when he found out that Beatrice's parents had already arranged a marriage for her, but thankfully, love conquered all. When "the crew" tried to execute their matrimonial plan, Beatrice sneaked out the side door of her home to the waiting arms of Leonardo.

In 1958, the two did exactly what fate had planned—they married and effortlessly devoted their lives and love to one another, to their beautiful children, his "Diddies" as he called them: Luci, Lori and Bart, and eventually to his "little Nonno's," James, Lucas, Ty, Colin, Bella and Olivia, all of which could be blanketed under one term: "Leo the Barber's Children."

The South Windsor Barber Shop became Leonardo's literal epicentre for haircuts, storytelling and soul-saving in 1967. Leonardo had actually wanted to become a doctor but decided to apply his "degree of being a good man" to an equally inspiring vocation. Leonardo was a 7 a.m. to 7 p.m. artist whose chair became your throne, giving first haircuts that led to prom haircuts, which led to "she dumped me" haircuts, which led to "she loves me" wedding haircuts. Then a literal, lather, rinse, repeat as he welcomed in the next generation of squirmy little fellows. He cared for up to five generations of families, feeling blessed to do so.

Leonardo's days off were equally devoted to humanity and community. His vibrant spirit was felt at hospitals and nursing homes where he shared kind words and listened with the same kindness while cutting hair for anyone who needed it. Sometimes it was their last haircut.

Everyone has a different sense of currency. Leonardo's currency was more evolved than mere dollars and cents. His currency was about the exchange of goodwill and benefit to mankind.

Our lives are made up of a sequence of moments. Leonardo created moments that nestled into your soul. There are countless stories of Leonardo's generosity that people have the privilege to share with each other and Leonardo's family. Stories about how when sickness fell upon them, Leonardo rallied. He could, of course, give a haircut and a shave, but what he truly gave was copious amounts of grace.

The term "you can get me later" was frequently spoken and gospel when it came from this man renowned for his impeccable integrity and loyalty. Leonardo valued your family and your needs, as if you were one of his own. This man was noble, incredibly silly, grateful and a whole lot of fun.

Together with Beatrice, Luci, Lori and Bart, they'd grab a bucket of KFC and head to Holiday Beach on Wednesdays, or Caboto Beach on Sundays. Family meals were an adventure, and the doors were always open for company. Leonardo kindly warned the neighbourhood boys of the "camouflaged tomato worms that bore fangs at night" should anyone creep into his garden. He also had the power to make your wheelchair vanish when he danced with you at a wedding.

No one was invisible through Leonardo's eyes, and every underdog learned to be a superhero when Leonardo showed you your cape. When you walked into his Curry Avenue bungalow, he was waiting for each one of you. Countless stories, tales of his grandchildren's baseball victories and jokes were shared, complete with hand gestures and belly laughs. James, Lucas, Ty, Colin, Bella and Olivia embraced not only their Nonno's advice on love, they took it on the chin when Leonardo would accuse them of cheating in a late-night game of scopa. Leonardo's devilish giggle was the undeniable clue that always gave him away as the trickster. If you were there, he was elated to rave about his new grand-furbaby or a recent conquest over a small engine repair that was getting the best of his patience. Until finally, it was time for wine and more wine.

The regulars, like Bruno, a true-blue Paisano since he first sat in Leonardo's chair in 1971, are just one of the many fellow-journeyers within the life and times of Leonardo Santamaria's playbook. Leonardo's pranks, his own laughter at his own pranks, his lawnmower obsession and his "uh oh, looks like we have a leak in the roof" impromptu showers, just barely scratch the surface of the man we now understand to be a legend.

We could say that Leonardo was a meticulous barber, an extraordinary "putzer and fixer" of literally everything. We could say he was a green thumb thanks to his father-in-law that he loved so tremendously. We could say that he was a great wine maker (also thanks to his father-in-law), and that Leonardo was born to entertain, whether that be by sharing his season tickets to Spitfire games, bowling on Thursday nights then heading to the Knights of Columbus after, taking friends to Tigers, Wings and Blue Jays games. But what we are really saying is that Leonardo was a rockstar at the art of being a good human being.

In April of 2010, a momentous occasion finally arrived: Leonardo, the master barber, retired after an illustrious career spanning an incredible 66 years. His unwavering dedication and tireless efforts had paved the way for a legacy that would be remembered for generations to come. As he swept the last of the hair from his beloved barber chair, Leonardo's heart swelled with pride and nostalgia. But, amidst the bittersweet feelings, he had one final request—a plea to all to ensure the special promises he had made to his clients remain honoured. These sacred vows, spoken in confidence, were not to be broken under any circumstance.

Leonardo's eyes sparkled with a fierce passion as he gazed upon the faces of his loyal clients, each one a testament to the unwavering commitment he had shown to his craft. As he bid them farewell, he knew that his legacy would live on through their stories, and that his dedication to his work would continue to inspire and ignite the flames of passion in the hearts of future barbers for generations to come.

Leonardo and Beatrice had a bond that was simply magical. So, when Beatrice was admitted to the Villages of St. Clair Long Term Care facility for 17 long months, Leonardo refused to leave her side. He spent every moment by her bedside, showing unwavering commitment and undying love.

On Sept. 13, 2019, Beatrice earned her wings, and at that very moment of separation, Leonardo's heart sustained an irreparable fracture. Just three months later, he received a pacemaker and stents. In March of the following year, he had a valve replacement and Leonardo made a formidable recovery.

Leonardo's passion for his garden filled his soul and helped him process the emptiness he felt without Beatrice. Despite the achy arthritis in his knees, he continued to tend to his assortment of plants, nurturing them with care and dedication. His home, where he had lived since 1958, was his sanctuary and his garden a reflection of how everything Leonardo touched simply became more beautiful.

On Sept. 27, just after the one-year mark of losing Beatrice, Leonardo made his way to Como's pizza, driven by a deep sense of gratitude for the staff at the Villages of St. Clair. He had never forgotten their kindness and was driven by a force within to remind them of their beautiful place they hold in the world.

The very next day, Leonardo called an ambulance for himself. He had a premonition that something was not right and took proactive steps. These steps were likely more to do with the concern he had for his family than directly about him. Later that day, he suffered a heart attack that kept him hospitalized for several days.

Just as autumn was beginning to show its beautiful colours one October morning, Leonardo passed away, finally joining his beloved Beatrice, the greatest love of his life.

As his loved ones mourned his passing, they also celebrated his life, filled with kindness and love. And when they were asked how they were doing, they'd say, "I am good, but I lie."

> *"Let us be grateful to the people who make us happy; They are the charming gardeners who make our souls blossom."*
> *~ Marcel Proust*

CHAPTER THREE

MAX MCMULLIN

The Guitar Sang Him to the Stars

Reflecting on the sacredness of the moment, the celebration of Max's life at the family farm was truly heaven on earth. The farm was alive in itself, with each barn board having been held, hoisted and a prideful shelter to generations of livestock, farm equipment, and cold beer on a hot summer's day. If a soul could be seen, this farm allowed you to see Max's.

Max was the youngest of 5 siblings who all shared the story of him ruining Christmas as they were whisked off to the hospital that snow-filled morning. Dad, Max Sr., now a brilliant 90 years young, still wearing his Levi's held up by a faded leather belt permanently crimped by a twine cutting knife nestled in its charcoal case, smiled warmly as he remembered his namesake nearly making his appearance in the old Ford. "Ford", a name that would have been bestowed upon baby Max should he not "hurry the hell up," as a heavily panting Dee bellowed, knowing that the grand finale to their family was arriving faster than what speedometer promised to arrive at the local hospital.

Max might have been the youngest, but he was by far not the meekest. By 2 years old, he was on skates pushing milk cartons around the family ice rink nestled to the side of the paddock, which conveniently served as not only a coat rack when the boys worked up a sweat but also the brakes for "Max on the move."

The bush behind the barn called to the boys often. It was the classroom of life. Max had wilderness in his blood, choosing to camp out under the stars for as long as the seasons allowed. He would often say he was going to serenade the critters, which meant his guitar was strapped to his back as he headed for his favourite oak stump stage, supporting his foot-stompin' bluesy country talents. He was beautiful beneath the stars—just ask Linda. At 17, she, too, was seduced by the energy of nature, with that same bush being her exhale retreat. Her quarter horse, Pebbles, insisted on discovering a new trail one early May evening just after dinner. Soon, she heard the faint sounds of a guitar and a voice that melted her in minutes. It took less than a handful of exchanged smiles for the two to fall in love, Linda reminisced from her tear drenched lips.

Sharing the same birthday, Max and Linda wed on Christmas day 1984 to make the perfect trifecta. The reception was held in the barn with strolls into the magic forest, which glistened with snow that seemed to have silver within its umbrella-sized flakes. Max and Linda built a home next door to his parents, and kept the same ice rink going for their three boys, Sean, Seth and Liam, who arrived within the first five years of their marriage. They were a family of nature and music, with the two concepts synonymous. Max taught all of his sons to play the guitar; however, they never lost sight of the music that echoed within the pervasive sounds of life emanating from the forest, which remained witness to this family's journey.

Max's life was a symphony of nature and love. He possessed an innate connection with the world around him, finding solace and inspiration in the embrace of the wilderness. He would spend countless hours exploring the nearby forests, climbing towering trees, and traversing hidden paths. His children all followed in his footsteps, their tiny hands clasped in his, as they discovered the wonders of nature together. They would chase butterflies, listen to the melodic songs of birds, and marvel at the vibrant hues of wildflowers. Max's family was his sanctuary, and every moment spent with them was a treasure etched in his heart.

It was within his heaven of the forest that Max's giant heart fell quiet, long before anyone was ever ready to say goodbye. At 55 years old, he was beaming with life, adventure, and love. Max left a hole that was impossible to fill. Linda was lost on how to say goodbye. How does one allow the man that is within the trees, the grass and the weathered wood to leave? Every celebration has always been imprinted on this land. His life was visible everywhere.

And so it happened that the Celebration of Max's life filled every blade of grass, echoed through the trees, penetrated the pores of the soil, the knots in the barnboard, and the souls of his family. The air was layered with his gentle energy, like soft cotton. His presence pulsated through the hearts of his loved ones, rolling down their cheeks directly towards their hearts.

And then there was the guitar. Max's guitar was poetry unto itself, its strings singing his gentle spirit to the stars above.

"A walk in nature, walks the soul back home"
~ Mary Davis

CHAPTER FOUR

ISABELLE GAUDETTE

Saving the Day in a Cardigan

On October 10, 1928, Isabelle burst onto the world stage, radiating kindness with the sweetest passion. She lived life like a superhero, but with the humble disguise of cozy cardigans.

Affectionately known as "Izzy," she was the embodiment of cool and understood the essence of life. Her journey began with a formidable British mother, who, after divorcing Izzy's abusive father, raised her with a stern hand. But Izzy knew in her heart that this wouldn't be the story of her life. Instead, she set her sights on what truly mattered: love, laughter, and a sense of belonging. For her, life was all about spreading kindness, sharing joy, and giving that special wink across the table to remind you that you were exactly where she wanted you to be.

If you were blessed to have met her, you were forever inspired. Izzy was cellular sweetness. Her timeless presence made her twinkle with a feeling of "home." During the day, she was a teacher, instilling good graces and phonics to her grade one students, which periodically included one of her eight children. If your mom was your teacher, you called her mom. Izzy was always a mom first.

Izzy seemed to pass through the years without ever aging. It was truly remarkable. Always the same sweet smile and demeanor that made you exhale the second she entered your sphere. It's as if her nurturing spirit and spot on sense of humour were her home-grown fountain of youth. Makeup never made it into her world, and thank goodness, because that glow was too darling to dull.

This woman was the sunflower representation of a human. She faced life with every ounce of love she had soaked into her soul. When times became tough, she turned herself towards others, ensuring her light could be easily absorbed.

At 74 years young, she lost her husband. His name is too cute to not mention. Elf was the lucky man to waltz her down the aisle on Aug. 6, 1944. They were both gorgeous and spunky. Once Tim, Joe, Alan, Jamie, Mary, Pauline, Geoff and Kathy arrived, the house on Eden Dr. was an adventure to behold.

Elf earned his wings in 2002 when he was 76 years young. He was renowned for his comical, yet steadfast beliefs in UFOs, healing pyramids and his words of wisdom such as, "I could wish for your health, I could wish for your wealth, but all I will wish for you is happiness because then you will gain all three."

Many people become stagnant after losing their life partner, waiting for the next talk show to come on or for promised visits from the family. Not our Izzy. She found her mojo, and she found Vegas. She wasn't alone, of course; her family always kept her at the centre of their lives. Izzy was the antithesis of the burden she often worried that she was. Rather, she was the centrepiece of all things exceptionally fun.

There are so many things to be said about Izzy. How she carried herself like poetry. She was Carol Burnett, Betty White, Mario Andretti and your Fairy Godmother all wrapped up into a truly beautiful and inspiring soul. She was care—the noun, the verb and the adjective.

Izzy was the listener, the adventurer, the giggler, the Sunday morning breakfast buddy, and the one that did not miss a beat when nonsense came knocking.

At 93 years young, still thriving independently, yet driving frightfully, Izzy was fortunate enough to join her family for Canadian Thanksgiving. A few board games under her belt complemented by a nip of wine, then Izzy was on her way. Of course, a zillion pictures were then taken and now treasured.

This lady wasn't a high-maintenance gal, no siree. Her joy in life came from her brood of eight kiddos, 21 grandkids, and 16 great-grandkids whom she adored with all her heart. Oh, and let's not forget every single person who gushed, "You were the absolute best teacher I've EVER had!" Izzy gained a country's worth of fans born from her 42 years of classroom creativity.

This shining spirit adored her freedom and never took the blessing of a long and healthy life for granted. On Nov. 5, 2021, Izzy shared a brief phone call with her daughter, saying that she had just returned from the casino, joked about winning mere pennies at the penny slots, and that she was tired. Shortly thereafter, after spending 33,994 days touching more hearts than she could have ever conceived, Izzy took her last gentle breaths to rise to an even greater freedom.

Izzy absolutely was the standing ovation at the end of her play!

Each Christmas, Izzy's family will feel the absence of her at their celebrations, and will look for her in her favourite chair. They will yearn to hear her laugh or just a glimpse of the way the Christmas lights glistened on her silver hair.

They will also shed tears of gratitude for having been blessed with an incredible matriarch, one whose sparkle will continue to guide them through their lives. They will smile, knowing that Izzy has, once again tucked her Kleenex in the cuffs of her cardigan sleeves as she creates lesson plans of genuine joy on her cosmic blackboard.

"It's not easy being a mother. If it were, fathers would do it."
~ The Golden Girls

CHAPTER FIVE

THE LIFE OF RILEY

A Tail of Love

Well, my humans couldn't have picked a better name for me, 'cause boy did I live it!

The world shone a little brighter the day all my brothers and sisters and I arrived on Sept. 13, 2006. There were about eight of us, but I was by far the most adorable. Mom was a Labrador, and so was Dad, but he had some hound dog in him, so all of us puppers got extra-long ears and magnificent sniffing noses. We could sing ba-rooooooooo like rock stars!

One day, a human family came to visit us. I really liked them and showed them all of my smarts. I was jet black and the only one that still had blue eyes. They couldn't resist me, and I don't blame them. Soon, I went for my first car ride. Jaime, my new brother, held onto me in the back seat while Mom Kelly drove, and Kara, my new sister, kept reaching back from the passenger side to soak up my cuteness.

Kelly really liked it when I peed or pooped in the house at first because she'd scoop it up immediately (to save it, I'm presuming) then reward me with letting me outside. One day I pooped outside and I got a treat. I never got treats when I did it inside, so I outsmarted them and refused to ever do my business in the house again.

The human teen years were tough. Jaime and Kara interrupted so many of my deep snorey snoozes! Kelly always took me everywhere. She even insisted on loading me into the car in the wee hours to pick up Jaime or Kara. Sometimes Kelly would mumble about making them walk. Walk? She wanted to walk? I wanna walk too!!! Yippee!!!!

Throughout the years I got all kinds of nicknames. Of course, I learned to answer to all of them. I never stopped amazing myself or my humans! Kara was the one who made them up. She's so funny. I was Moofus, Moofonzio, Nation, FonzNation, Mudscup and sometimes Roo! I really liked the sound of their voices when they looked at me. It was almost as beautiful as the sound of a cheese wrapper opening from three rooms away with the music blaring loudly. Regardless, I would report to my kitchen post immediately!

Everyday I'd wake up and let them know how much I loved everyone. I took heroic steps to protect them, too. I'd always do my best to remember to rip open and scatter the garbage when they weren't home to make sure there were no dangers in there. If they went to Costco and bought bread or bagels, well, we all know carbs are the enemy. I made darn sure to swipe them off the counter as soon as I could and devour them in Mom's office. These acts of love were endless. There were ripple effects too—so much of what I did was to help Mom remember to vacuum!

I was also an extreme athlete. Tennis balls made me the happiest. I knew that every ball hockey game on the street was an invitation for me to take their ball and show them how fast I could run away with it. Did I mention I was also part porpoise? I saved so many sticks from Lake Erie, I should have probably been awarded a medal. And one time, in a very fleeting lapse of coordination, I fell off a boat in Lake Saint Clair and single-handedly fought off some very rude swans and geese!

Soon Mom and I moved to the waterfront and every day, a few times a day, I got to stroll by the most amazing scenery and snack on some goose droppings. It weirded Mom out. I wish Kelly was more adventurous. All of my new neighbours loved me and were amazed at how I remembered they kept treats in their pockets. I'd show them their pockets whenever I saw them just to make sure nothing went stale in there.

My purpose in this life was to fill Kelly's heart with love every day. She did the same for me. One day, I heard Kelly complaining that she was gaining weight. I then decided it was best to lie right in front of the fridge door when she was cooking or to listen for the toaster to pop and plot my thieving strategy. Riley, always to the rescue! I just loved her that much! Bottomless love to match my appetite! Afterwards I'd roll over like a walrus to allow Kelly to rub my belly. I'd smile, showing her my fancy little bottom teeth.

When Kelly bought her convertible VW beetle, I started touring the county in style. Kelly thought people were looking at the car (she's so naïve). I knew they were admiring me in all of my nobility as my ears danced in the wind!

A few days ago, I could no longer hide that my 12 years and 8 months of life were catching up to me. I kept it in for so long that Kelly was really upset when she saw me. We started to talk a lot with our eyes. I wanted her to know that I was going away, but my love wasn't. I wanted her to know that her friend Kathy is right, I will always lead the way for her. I wanted her to know that I will take a bit of her with me and leave a lot of me behind, so she is never really without me. I wanted her to know that she will see me again. I may look different and feel different but my spirit will be within.

On May 24, 2019, after a happy meal and milkshake in the park that I grew up in, the four of us, me, Jaime, Kara and Mom were together as we said goodbye, just like when we said hello.

"If there are no dogs in heaven, then when I die,
I want to go where they went"
~ Will Rogers

CHAPTER SIX

DON BISSON

A Poet & A Warrior

Don was iconic from birth. His presence, his vibe, if you will, unfolded layer by layer since he started having a few beers with his grandfather at 5 years old while watching the hockey game. Don was a beautiful mosaic of life. He was a "cowboy," born 200 years too late. He was a meaningful contrast in terms. In a 6'1" package that appeared much larger to most, Don was Rudyard Kipling, Alexander the Great, John Wayne and Fred Astaire, all rolled up into one comedic, "Weekend at Bernie's"-esque, get on his bike and head to the other side of the country, protector of all protectors, gentlemen. Don had a light that felt immortal to all of those that followed him into and throughout life.

Don was happiness. He was the "don't dwell on the problem" smile as you move to the solution and sing a little song as you tinker your way there. Don was sunshine. He warmed your spirit and cuddled your soul. He was an historian, never at a loss for an answer or a spark for another question. He was one of the deepest rivers you ever swam in. Don was a poet and a warrior who loved from his core and moved through life with a gentle reverence, concluding most drama with, "Ah, let's go have fun."

Don was a scholar, graduating from the trenches of the School of Hard Knocks. He waited 5 long years after arriving to his family on Nov. 18, 1952 to identify himself as a "carve your own path" flight risk. This became evident when he would escape from kindergarten and grade one, only to run home and seek refuge in the dog house. By the time his formative years arrived, he found himself learning his mathematics and grammar at Holy Rosary Grade School as he studied survival on the streets. You'd think he'd grow a shell and enter adulthood with a chip on his shoulder, but he was better than that. He had coached his brothers, who at six years old had to fight to claim their place on the mean streets of which they were raised, to "go for the nose." But he actually grew to detest bullying, and as the "Duke" of Douillard Rd, Don became a light warrior. No one, under his watch, would be disrespected nor hurt in any way, shape or form. Don's heart stretched for miles and heard everything.

Once his teenage years arrived, Don learned a multitude of things. It was likely that growing into the significance that he was destined for was often disarming, but he also discovered that he had rhythm within him. At 14 years old, his friend's mother got him up to dance and taught him the swagger of some moves. This most assuredly helped once he was able to head to the French-Canadian Club, where all the girls were lined up to glide along the dance floor with charismatic Don. In the meantime, he stayed true to his childhood goal shared with his brothers which was to "make Mom laugh." Oh, that noble woman, what she must have endured with those five clowns! Their skits, their she-nanigans, but most of all, their all-encompassing passion for loving life, loving each other and loving her. Momma Bisson did an amazing job.

Don was a fixer. At Ford Motor Co., he embraced his profession as a tool and die maker, happy to save the day along with his colleague Marcel. Don was precise, methodical and on-point with his expertise, always. He even whistled while he worked.

As a father, he was Mt. Everest with a smile. He taught his sons, Adrian and Ryan, some things through his words but most things through his example.

There are few people that we will meet in this world that can be defined the way Don can. Such beauty and strength rarely travel so deep. One time Don hit a golf ball so high into the air that it can be coined the "Sputnik" upon re-entry. Who else can elicit a smile just at the thought of him? Who else can likely shoot a dime spotted through his scope from miles away?

Who else can approach Joel Quenneville, Coach of the Chicago Blackhawks, and admit that he is the only French Canadian who knows nothing about hockey, only for Joel to say, "Neither do I." And then Don followed with, "Why are all your players Russian?" When Quenneville replied, "They're not," Don asked why all their names were "Forecheck."

Don was always at the end of the phone when you needed him. He was also at your side when he knew that was his place to be. When Linda, his friend, wife, kindred spirit, and biggest fan said, "You know, when you go hunting, I might go to the Camino Trail, I've always wanted to do that." He said, "I will be there by your side." And so, from Aug. 13 to Oct. 2, 2022, that is exactly what they did. For 38 days they talked, healed, shared their joined hearts, and explored not only their individual souls but those of other fellow journeyers. Once they arrived back home, a northern Quebec moose hunting trip was awaiting Don, and despite this nagging pain in his ribs, he went. Off the grid, brave as always, and never ever to disappoint those who depend on him. Sleeping proved difficult while he was away. Upright in a chair was his most comfortable remedy.

As soon as he returned home, it was evident time for care had arrived. A trip to the doctors was not enough. When Linda called the ambulance, Don was not combative, he was compliant. He knew this was bigger than him. And it was. The essence of both their beings seemed to drop into the abyss when the doctor shared with them, "Pancreatic cancer is a beast." It was a beast that was to rob Don of his ability to live, love and join his siblings as they dance around the newest potential members of the Bisson clan. An embarrassing tradition to all but the Bisson boys!

On Sunday, Nov. 6, 2022, Don shared, "This is the last day." He actually apologized that "this is taking so long." The forever protector, right? This meant it was his last day to share and care with a clear understanding. So, he met with everyone, separately. Those moments will never be lost; they're cellular.

On Nov. 11, 2022, always a day to pause in remembrance, Don took his last, agreed by all hearts that loved him, "too soon" breaths. He leaves behind a mind-blowing trail of love and a legacy that shines of hero proportions.

"There's nothing more powerful than a humble person with a warrior spirit who is driven by a bigger purpose."
~ Jeff Osterman

CHAPTER SEVEN

SARAH EDEN

Invisible Scars

On June 1, 1932 Sarah arrived to start a life that would strengthen her soul through the sharp edges of life lessons and fill her spirit by virtue of the love that finally found her. Less than one month before Sarah was born, Amelia Earhart flew her plane across the Atlantic. Most certainly some of Amelia's fierce woman magic dust was sprinkled on Sarah to help her get through the challenges that awaited.

At the age of 7, Sarah's father moved her from Minnesota to Texas, where he would drop Sarah off at a Convent that was virtually hidden behind its gnarled vines and shrouded trees. It would be difficult to imagine the multitude of emotions that Sarah felt as she tried to cope with the challenges to her emotional development at such a young age, while dealing with the fear and isolation that constantly threatened to derail her progress and prevent her from putting one foot in front of the other.

As a teenager, Sarah lived with a kind farming family during the week, allowing her to attend a local high school where the majority of the kids had milked a cow or cleaned a few stalls as the sun was alerting the roosters to sing "cock-a-doodle-doo." She also had the grace of several nuns that tucked Sarah under their wings, encouraging her to stay soft yet strong, to develop her skills, including her natural ability for music. Through this vessel of kindness, Sarah taught herself to play piano and to know that that person in the mirror was beautiful and worthy.

It was that fortitude that allowed her to dry her own tears as she spent her childhood Christmases all alone at the convent. Just Sarah and an assortment of 88 black and white keys that played a friendship melody to Sarah's soul.

In 1953, at 21 years old, Sarah met her first and only true love Sam, thanks to an introduction from friends. Marriage followed in 1955 as the two put down deep roots in a neighbourhood that became their village. They danced and sang in the streets to celebrate life, holidays, and each other. Their homes became the extended homes of the neighbourhood children. Everyone was safe and loved.

Sarah's spoonful of love and support from her youth now was an ocean in comparison. She never missed a day feeling blessed, and yet she never shared her painful past. Sarah used her past to help her appreciate her present. She did not demand a badge of honour, nor was pity ever to be her fallback plan. She had three amazing children to champion, and in just being her, she instilled a pride and peacefulness in each of their hearts.

Sarah was a woman who could patiently get to know people simply through observing them. She was intuitive, empathic, and, on every level, real. When she watched a movie, she looked for the meaning. Sarah embraced Christmas in the spirit that it was meant to be celebrated—sharing love, hope, and joy. She created a sea of presents for no other reason than it was the outward representation of her inward love and gratitude.

Sarah knew life was about lessons, so she remained a forever student, striving to thrive as a woman of kindness and altruism. Life began in so many ways when she had a family to call her own. She showered them with a love that now radiates like diamonds in their veins.

On a blustery winter's day in 2020, at 88 years young, this brave, sweet, selfless soul returned to Sam's waiting wings. She leaves behind a legacy that pulses with inspiration and a reminder that our struggles are not our shackles.

"My mission in life is not merely to survive, but to thrive; and to do so with some passion, some compassion, some humor, and some style."
- Maya Angelou

CHAPTER EIGHT

EVERYONE'S STORY

When Someone You Loved, But Didn't Like, Dies

It's an unfortunate, yet common, reality. Not everyone in your life played fair, right? Not every Dad was your hero and protector, and not every Mom wiped your tears, reminding you of your awesomeness. Your big brother was too stoned, or your twin sister was outrageously unlike you, except for her face. Stupid camouflage. You spent your lifetime loving someone for their defined role in your life despite their falling short, repeatedly, of what you actually needed from them to feel secure in this world.

You kept up appearances throughout your life, believing one of your grand successes was fooling the masses into believing you were a cog in the epitome of a millennium days Brady

Bunch family. The less questions, the better. Simply because you had no words to explain the truth.

Then, they die. The funeral comes, and you are supposed to feel devasted and lost. You try. You try hard. But in reality, you can't feel. This means you grieve twice—once for what you had and lost, and then again for what you needed, never got... and now, for sure, will never have. The only person you believed could fill your always-empty tank of love, acceptance, self-esteem, confidence, or belonging is now gone. That is what you are truly grieving. That is what you've always been grieving.

Your hope to heal has been deflated. Hijacking your spirit along with it. That is your truth.

Wrong! There you are standing. What you haven't realized is that all that you lacked, you've actually harvested from within you. Welcome to the "ruby red slippers" phenomenon.

So how do you handle it? You stop and acknowledge that through some backwards spin, that person gave you a strength, a perceptive ability, and a deeper connection to others. You are undoubtedly kinder, more intuitive, succinctly aware of lurking chameleons, and quietly appreciative of your newfound freedom.

Life is filled with its share of highs and lows, a constant interplay of light and darkness. It is within this rhythm that we uncover the strength of our resilience. Like a flexible stem swaying with the wind, we learn to adapt without breaking. When faced with challenges, such as the complicated emotions of losing someone we feel we never got it quite right with, our foundation is rocked.

The only thing left to do is say thank you and understand that not all lessons come with a pretty bow. You will be fine. Take some time to cry, to vent, to walk it off, and then move forward, leaving your once-needed armour behind.

"Someone I once loved gave me a box full of darkness. It took me years to understand that this, too, was a gift."
~ Mary Oliver

CHAPTER NINE

DEBBIE CLARKE

The Clear Bead

Debbie and Don were like two peas in a pod for a whopping 51 years! The lovebirds met in drama class and got hitched while still in their teens, on Nov. 6, 1971. They were so smitten with each other that they often hit up Zoro's Steak House in Toronto, where they had their honeymoon dinner, as many times as humanly possible.

So, if you ever find yourself at that steakhouse, be sure to mention this iconic duo, and you'll be in for a treat! They'll probably regale you with tales of their teenage love, and maybe even give you some tips on how to keep a relationship spicy after all these years.

Debbie was a signature arrival with her beautiful fingernails and her less than salon perfect hair.

Her life-long love and selfless volunteering to Riverside Skating Club, Riverside Competitive Bursary, Sun Parlour Region, Western Ontario Sectional Championships, By-law committees and Skate Canada were badges of love she wore with incredible humility.

While we can marvel at the generosity of time and incredible devotion all of these roles represented, the big question is "why?" Why does someone take on all of this? With such passion and drive!

Likely, it is because Debbie, for many years of her life, might have felt that she was just a clear colour on a beaded string, holding space for others to be admired and supported, sometimes only noticed by chance and never really held to the light of all possibilities or cradled in the nurturing hands of promise.

In her own distinct way, Debbie managed to turn the spotlight of love to as many aspiring youths as possible, to fuel their dreams and, above all, let them know that they were seen.

On Jan. 5, 2023, Debbie celebrated her 70th galivant through the calendars. Her formative years were spent in Windsor, Ontario where she graduated from Gordon McGregor, Brennan, Commerce and the School of Life. A born administrator, she gravitated to careers in veterinary offices such as Forest Glade and Clearwater, where she made sure the day-to-day operations ran smoothly, and a few cute kitties found their way home with her at the end of the day.

Later, Debbie became an integral part of co-op housing, earning a reputation for her generous spirit as she helped people find homes. This kindness was reciprocated by random gifts that would show up at her family's doorstep. Although Debbie briefly dabbled in property management, her true passion was always her love for ice rinks.

Debbie relished every opportunity to mingle with those who played a pivotal role in fostering promise and pride. Whether she was rooting for her daughter Trish in competitions, vociferously shouting at her son Gary or grandson Jackson's hockey games, or imbuing faith in Tessa Virtue & Scott Moir, and Jennifer Robinson, figure skating champions, while chaperoning them on their ascent to Olympic stardom, Debbie served as the liaison between them all.

She passionately embodied the role of a second mother to numerous young souls who were fortunate enough to have her nurturing presence in their lives. She was the legendary Momma "C" who spread her wings of love and guidance over them with fervor and dedication.

Have you ever heard the phrase "pressure makes diamonds?" It comes from the fact that coal, which is dark and dirty, when under pressure for a long period of time, turns into diamonds, one of our most valued jewels. The same is true of the human being. When we put our muscles under regular stress, they grow. When our immune system faces challenges, it becomes stronger. And when we face challenges in life, and approach them with the belief that they can make us more psychologically resilient, that's exactly what happens. Debbie was no stranger to challenges in life.

Despite being raised by a single mother and struggling to find a sense of belonging, she also persevered through numerous health challenges, including four knee replacements, several blood clots, two neck fusions, two back fusions, a fall on the driveway in bitter cold weather, osteoporosis, fibromyalgia, a broken leg, and a significant internal bleed from a minor bump.

Every single day, she faced challenges that varied in size and shape, working very hard to become the best version of herself. And on those exceptional days, she achieved remarkable feats such as transforming lasagna with Cheese Whiz into a gourmet dinner or discovering a secure hideaway to savour cabbage rolls, so Don's keen sniffer couldn't detect the aroma.

Debbie and Don were the perfect pair, their love and balance unrivaled. Except when it came to Debbie's sneaky shopping. She was notorious for adhering to a 'two of everything, price tags are irrelevant" spending spree. This theme also fuelled her wrapping paper addiction. In addition to Jackson, Debbie's other grandchildren, McKayla and Alyssa were going to be set to unwrap gifts till they had kids of their own!

As days turned into months, Don was an unwavering pillar of support for Debbie as her strength gradually diminished. With a fierce determination, he made sure to never miss a moment to attend to her needs and was by her side until her very last breath, pouring all his heart into giving her just a few more precious moments and letting her know how much she was loved.

Then, on that fateful Friday of Jan. 27, 2023, Debbie was finally released from the confines of her body, free to soar to the great rink in the sky, where she would undoubtedly raise a glass of Chardonnay and continue to inspire and uplift all those who held her close to their hearts to reach for their dreams and make them a reality.

Once Debbie arrived at the pearly gates, we bet she took one look around and thought, "This place could use a little sprucing up." We can just picture her with her trusty clipboard and signature broach, ready to join every committee possible and categorize everything to perfection. Even in the afterlife, Debbie will make sure everything runs smoothly!

"What counts in life is not the mere fact that we have lived. It is what difference we have made to the lives of others that will determine the significance of the life we lead."
~ Nelson Mandela

CHAPTER TEN

JASON FINDLEY

A Shadow Between the Cracks

Jason was born in the wee hours of a spring morning. His curly auburn locks, green eyes tinged with innocence, and a heart filled with forgiveness would be challenged even before his first steps were taken. As the youngest in a family already mosaiced with father figures and step siblings, it was no place to be when your existence required unwavering nurturance.

Changing schools was not the answer, but it was the only attempt. Not all teachers were "out to get him," and not all kids wanted to bully him. The fact was, Jason was awkward and remedial; yet, had the gentlest heart that only saw love through his puppy-like personality. His teens were treacherous as he was never supported to find his own tribe. He could solve math equations like a wizard, but floundered in friendships. His spirit shrivelled as his hand desperately reached out between the cracks for just one person to hold on. One person to be kind.

Jason needed a hero. He deserved a hero.

Just as Plato said, "At the touch of love, everyone becomes a poet", Jason was a canvas just waiting to reveal his artwork.

At 23, Jason was diagnosed with high functioning autism. With this tattered label now affixed to him, he yearned to salvage his pieces that had fallen between those life-sucking cracks. Where was his confidence? Did that slip away before his self-worth? What about belonging and self-actualization? In the triangle of Maslow's hierarchy of needs, Jason was a square.

Within those dark recesses where he searched for himself, he discovered something that, for at least a short while, made him feel euphorically content. As the real world's jagged edges continued to impale him, drugs filled the holes. Finally, whether on purpose, by accident, or just merely a manoeuvre of surrender, Jason's 25-year-old heart was stopped by fentanyl.

There are more Jasons out there. Let's lean in together and help them find their way out of the shadows.

> *"The attempt to escape from pain, is what creates more pain."*
> *~ Gabor Maté*

CHAPTER ELEVEN

ROSE MARIE TENNANT

The Wealth of a Mother's Love

The words I heard from Debbie about her mom were kind, proud, worrisome, fun-loving, crazy, creative, flirty, compassionate, strong, traveler, animal lover and just one amazing woman who had a knack of making you feel complimented when she called you an asshole. Rose Marie was a woman who knew how to love, create, pull people together with her charisma, and explore each corner of what life had to offer with unrivaled pizzazz.

Born in Windsor, Ontario, on Aug. 1, 1930, Rose Marie began her ambitious and adventuresome life with her family on Tecumseh Road. She attended St. Genevieve, the Adult retraining center, and then transitioned to a position at the Windsor Airport where she worked in the foreign money exchange and post office. It was really there that she got her start to a career that would allow her dynamic personality and sociable spirit to soar.

Rose Marie was hired to work at the Shopper's Drug Mart post office, and became a legendary fixture there. You just didn't go there to mail a letter, oh no, not on Rose Marie's watch. With her trademark gigantic earrings on, she would convince young children that an itty bitty someone lived in her mailbox, and this friendly character had a direct link to Santa. In front of the children, she'd have a discussion with this mysterious character and ultimately convince the children to lean into the opening of the mailbox to discuss their wish list for Santa. By this time, they were sure they had the ear of Santa's right-hand man, and all their wishes would be granted. Of course, this would then be applied to the Easter Bunny as well. Rose Marie wasn't merely just an advocate for the kiddies—on Senior's Day, she would create games and dress up in one of her homemade costumes. Elvira was a real hit!

When Debbie, her only child was about 10 years old, Rose Marie's first husband John passed away. Very shortly after, Rose Marie was told that the owners of the house they lived in wanted her to move out immediately. Through an act of tremendous kindness, she was offered another house to live in. A house that was shy of a few things…. such as plumbing. Rose Marie rose to the occasion and found a way to make bathing in a large metal tub not only feel normal, but fun, to her young daughter. During the day she sewed clothes for Debbie's Barbies, and at night, she was likely hiding her tears as she tossed and turned, worrying about providing for herself and her sweet little girl. But basking in her mother's determined provision, Debbie only felt pure love and incredible devotion.

Everyone knew the truth; Rose Marie was a going concern. She had her hand in everything and added joy to lives she likely had no idea she even touched. Much of her magic occurred on the dance floor. With a few ballroom dance lessons under her belt and many hours spent cutting the rug at Lansbury Park, she turned herself into a national talent and began competing. Rose Marie used to go out dancing with her sister Alma and Alma's husband Joe to a bar. It was there that a young man named Joe Tennant noticed her and began to court her. However, as a mother first, Rose Marie waited almost eight months before allowing him the privilege of meeting Debbie.

Soon they were married, moved to Byng St. in Windsor, and grabbed ahold of life with both hands. The happy trio would travel to PEI, California, entertain 20-30 people in their small but loved-filled home. Rose Marie was game for everything, always expanding her comfort level. Amongst those "everythings" were Tai Chi at the riverfront, knitting, macramé, stained glass creations and endless everyday sewing of cute-beyond-words Easter bonnets and dress creations. She'd start baking a month before Christmas, making 2 or 3 desserts a night, and never left out a delicacy that resembled candied strawberries. Rose Marie's talents turned a teeny-tiny trailer into a vacation destination designer utopia. She had no limits and clearly saw the world in technicolour.

She was tricky too! Their home on Byng Rd. needed some work done to a ceiling. After feeling she had asked her husband too many times to take care of the repair, she decided to take a broom to the ceiling. Everyday she'd increase the damage just a little bit more until he asked what on earth was happening. Her words were, "Just fix it." It's likely that when he did embark on the repairs, she celebrated by dyeing her hair yet another new colour.

All this time she was still going to work and loving her job at Shopper's. One day, however, she had car trouble during her commute and had to leave her car at the side of the road. Of course, there were no cell phones then, so she began the trek to work on foot. As she passed by Powers Motorcycle, someone came out and asked her if she was okay. Next thing you know, Rose Marie is on the back of a Harley getting chauffeured to work. Often after that, they'd pop by her house and take her for more rides. She was hooked and did all that she could to convince her husband, John, that she needed a Harley, too.

In 1985 at the age of 55, Rose Marie lost her husband John, and once again, she was on her own. Six years prior to this, in 1978, she had suffered a heart attack and was showing the very early signs of dementia. But was that going to stop her? Well, that's a rhetorical question at this point. Rose Marie lived a

"Carpe Diem" life. She returned to going to dances, making many new friends, and continued to embrace the ones that were always there for her. One of her friend's sons owned a limo business, so a group of the gals would jump into a limo, head out on the town, only to be picked up and chauffeured home in style. Rose Marie did not need to drink to enjoy herself. All of her shenanigans were done blissfully sober.

After enjoying a trailer in Lakeland, Florida with her friend Maurice, Rose Marie, continued to travel and eventually purchased a trailer and condo closer to her loved ones. Her aim was to reduce her responsibilities and bring more ease into her life. Despite adopting a new lifestyle, her superstitions persisted, just like her daughter Debbie's. Hence, one must refrain from opening an umbrella or putting new shoes on the table in their homes. In case of any salt spills during brunches, it is customary to throw a dash over each shoulder. Also, it was always best to keep black cats away from her path.

As health and cognitive issues began to impede Rose Marie's daily functioning, she transitioned to the Royal Marquis Retirement home, then ultimately to Extendicare Southwood Lakes for the last 8 years of her life. Her best friends were, as always, her daughter and fierce advocate Debbie, and a cute little tan and white robotic cat, lovingly called "Baby" or "Asshole." For the most part, Rose Marie was not aware that this cat, which responded with movements just like a real cat, was not a real cat...and so it currently has jam stains on it from when Rose Marie would feed it.

Rose Marie was a presence here on earth for 88 magnificent years and most certainly added sunshine to heaven.

"I had two mothers, two mothers I claim.
Two different people, yet with the same name.
Two separate women, diverse by design
But I loved them both, because they were both mine.
The first was the mother, who carried me here.
Gave birth and nurtured, and launched my career.
She was the one whose features I bear.
Complete with the facial expression I wear.
She gave me some music, which follows me yet
Along with examples in life that she set.
Then as I grew older, she some younger grew,
And we'd laugh as just mothers and daughters can do.
But then came the year that her mind clouded so,
And I sensed that the mother I'd known soon would go
So quickly she changed, and turned into the other –
A stranger who dressed in the clothes of my mother.
Oh, she looked just the same, at least at arm's length.
But, she was the child now, and I was her strength.
We'd come full circle, we women three.
My mother the first, the second, and me.
And together, there is nothing but love which is how it will al-
ways be."
~ Joann Snow Duncanson

CHAPTER TWELVE

DAN RAHM

Rules to Live By, Or Have Fun Breaking

D o you remember when you were a kid and you would lie on the dewy grass of summer, gazing up towards the sky to find the pictures that would magically form before your curious eyes? Most of us smile as we reminisce about those gentle times, unfortunately acknowledging that our wonder of the world was replaced with adult demands.

Dan never lost that gift, that amazement, the love of the special touch of turning imagination into creation. Dan was an observer of life and curator of smiles. He left us a treasure map to guide us through the rest of our lives. So, we are going to look at Dan's life through his wise words left in "Rahm's Rules."

Dan began his exploration of life on April 30, 1951 in Leamington, Ontario. The pronunciation of his last name is "raam"....thankfully, not Ron. There would have been a huge betrayal of Dan's number one rule: "Never trust anyone with two first names."

He left the pitter patter of his curious feet in a tiny town named Blytheswood. The energy of his ambition surely still echoed in the halls when his school was torn down only to be replaced by the Moose Lodge, and then the Scholar's Restaurant. After graduating high school, Dan did venture off to St. Clair College but the allure of watching Devonshire Mall being constructed proved too much for his thirsty left-brain engineering mind. He wanted to take it all in, so he then executed his second rule: "If you want to see farther, lean forward."

The mall watching won, but that didn't stop him from his insatiable need to feel accomplished at the end of a day. So, he enrolled in distance learning, and over the span of 10 years, he graduated from a 4th Class Power Engineer, to a 1st Class Engineer, writing 8 exams each time to transition forward.

Dan earned every ticket possible and became a literal master of all trades. His career path began at Freedlands with his best friend Fred as his boss. To avoid Fred firing him, again, Dan moved to Heinz where he would spend the next 45 years, ultimately becoming the manager of the Powerhouse.

Dan afforded each young buck that came under his supervision an opportunity to prove themselves. He lived by his next rule, a rule he instilled on his family as well: "It doesn't matter how other people work, Rahms keep their head down and put in an honest day's work." To drive this home to his subordinates, he liked to remind them that "your way is okay, but we WILL do it my way."

Dan loved to love. His true north of love was his wife, Joyce. A blind date the summer of 1976, complete with brutal lamb-chops at the Hacienda restaurant and Dan's "Jumping Jack Flash" dance moves at a bar later on, likely sealed the love deal which brought them straight to the altar at Leamington's Gold-smith Church on June 17, 1978.

A Niagara Falls honeymoon followed immediately, where Dan embodied his inner Chevy Chase. He toured the town in his tuxedo shoes and shorts. His eyes always told the story of his next comic maneuvers. It's likely many unsuspecting tourists were enlightened by Dan's spontaneous sense of humour, com-plete with his Rahm Rule: " If you want to really add a punchline to your joke, finish it off with a kidney shot to the listener."

Hwy #77 became the Rahms forever home. It was there Joyce not only raised her 3 children, Lisa and Aaron (Dan was included in the count), but she also worked together with Dan to build an entire second story to their home. They likely needed the extra room to store Dan's vast collection of jeans and coats. During the construction Dan held true to his Rahm Rule of thumb when fixing things: "Anything can be fixed with three main tools ~ screwdriver (no matter the drill bit), silicone and dryer hose."

The Rahm home was an oasis, pristine in its gardens and rich in "shoot the shit" laughter with Dan's buddy, Larry. It would have put most hardware stores to shame, having every modified tool imaginable. It established itself in the same way a lending library recycles murder mystery novels.

Dan was a tinkerer that made things out of strange things. Even if it was a new thing, he held true to his Rahm Rule: "Only read the instructions when all else fails."

The backyard served as the command centre for the covert operations known as, "Don't tell Mom." Nineteen-foot boats were hidden, potato guns were created, and maybe, just maybe, he was listening to his Patsy Cline or Belinda Carlyle CDs, since even the thief that broke into his little red sportscar was too proud to take them.

His 58 itemized, likely Debbie Travis paint cans were stored properly, with Dan insisting her brother, Randy Travis, would be proud. "PS: Don't tell Mom the truth about that either; she is really buying my bull!"

Dan was a plethora of wisdom and wit. No one will ever buy a newspaper the same way when you accept his next 'Rahmism': "Never ever purchase the newspaper on top." Keep in mind that he did have an uncanny practice of doing everything that he told others not to do. He walked by his own beat, but would check up on others often. If he felt you were lying, his next rule came into play: "If you want to tell if someone is lying, have them look you in the eye and say all of the following words, "Black squirrel" without laughing."

On Valentine's Day of 2019, after a year of concern, Dan was diagnosed with prostate cancer. In his family's words, he didn't miss a beat. The courage and resilience he exhibited, well, it was not surprising, just as it will be forever inspiring. When the cancer invaded his bones, a fall caused his neck to break. Only Dan would be interviewing the doctors during the surgery about their tools and likely making suggestions on how to modify them. When they were attaching the halo to his skull, I wonder if he shared his Rahm rule: "There is no need for multiple screwdriver bits. Just pick your favourite and jam it into the screw until it works."

From the moment that Dan entered this world, he literally rained sunshine (or toothpaste spit if you were his sister Judy) on every person he touched. He dodged crushed marshmallow cookies to double up on butter tarts, and he cheered on the Detroit Red Wings, while secretly crushing on the Toronto Maple Leafs. When he took his last peaceful breaths on Dec. 15, 2019 after sharing 68 years of great love, unprecedented laughter and inspiration, Dan had one more trick up his sleeve.

Dan and Joyce's 42nd wedding anniversary would have been June 15, 2020. Dan had been a less than romantic gift giver. Car parts, tires, and garage trinkets had been his theme for their 41 years together, but boy, oh boy, did he make up for it once he earned his wings.

On that very day, Joyce received a call from the Princess Margaret Home Lottery Corporation in Toronto telling her that she was the lucky winner of a beautiful Muskoka cottage. Hence a new Rahm Rule: "A Rahm in love is a Rahm lucky with love."

"Everyone wants to live on top of the mountain, but all the happiness and growth occurs while you're climbing it."
~Andy Rooney

CHAPTER THIRTEEN

CEDAR RIVERS

A Heart Filled with Hope

Cedar was an enigma, especially to herself, since birth. When she found the yellowed copy of her birth announcement that read 5lbs _ ozs, she understood that her life would be a series of mysteries that she'd bravely seek to solve. Cedar was kind, a gentle spirit trapped in an opposing world. She wanted to embody a Pitbull but was far more of a Golden Retriever trapped in a Jack Russell frame.

As an infant, Cedar's parents kept her in a make shift baby basket on the dining room table. Next to Cedar, also on display, were the plastic fruit and the pet turtles. The turtles, Tom and Jerry, often were found on their passage to freedom, clinging to the back of the curtains. How much time they spent as roomies with Cedar will likely never be known.

Her home, the bricks and mortar of it, was stunning. Her family were the leaders of affluence in a budding neighbourhood. Disingenuous smiles, inground swimming pools and Lincolns were aplenty. A bank balance of pretend happiness.

She lived in two complete worlds, she felt. In the visible world, she was a contender. Cedar was easily a straight A student, cute as a button, and athletic in every sport from baseball to spelling bees. She made friends easily and was the forerunner of the buzz word, "unconditional." In grade school, she mingled with every clique. Cedar was like salt, a hint of her added flavour to the mix.

Home life was different. Lunch breaks included a walk home with friends to their respective homes. Oftentimes, Cedar would just wander around the neighbourhood until the time was right to head back to school. Lunchtime felt risky for her. Either the door to her house would be locked, or her mother was on her fifth rye and something, or if Cedar was lucky, her mother was channelling her best June Cleaver routine. Regardless, Cedar kept her head down and smile up.

When holidays came, it was like Miss Manners, Martha Stewart & Attila the Hun were running the show. Cedar's Mom, Janet, was brilliant, beautiful and likely in need of a psychiatric assessment. The polished household was a rarely visited pretty prison. Yet somehow, Christmas marked the occasion where Uncle "So & So" along with Aunt "Where'd you come from" arrived for the big family feast. Janet was a remarkable cook and hostess. Cedar was the frightened show pony. If a photo was taken, it would look like a commercial. If audio was added, it was like the Walton's were on acid.

Her Dad, Charlie, seemed to always have a pressing meeting to dash out to. He wasn't a bad guy. He was kind, charismatic and well-liked. He did his best to create redeeming moments in the family. Charlie coached several of Cedar's sports teams and was honestly, from what she saw, doing his best. Charlie and Janet were toxically estranged the entirety of Cedar's life despite putting on the good show when it counted.

Cedar made her way through high school as awkwardly poised as most teenagers do. Everyone thought she was happy, but she had a six pack of survival muscles knotted within. The time had come where she stopped inviting friends home. Daily, she sprayed "Loves Baby Soft" on her clothes to mask the smell of her parents' offensive cigarette smoke, and she accepted any friend's offer to stay for dinner. Otherwise, she'd grabbed some crackers and head to her room.

Her high school graduation came and went. The awards she earned would be mailed because attending meant the display of her dysfunctional family. Cedar wasn't wired for such a humbling moment in a world where her friends all seemed to be rooted in Hallmark family moments.

As soon as she could, garbage bags proved perfect for pseudo luggage. She didn't take much. All she really had of value was what felt like a fragmented version of herself.

Ambitious to her core, she made her way through Simon Fraser University to become a journalist, where the world unfolded before her eyes like a brilliant lotus flower.

Cedar spent the next 15 years of her life reporting on world events and chronicling the most delicious life encounters, from heroism to humility. She never lost touch with her parents yet chose to make her visits brief. She adopted the 'rushing out to a meeting' code of coping.

Within the same year, both of her parents passed away. It was bittersweet. A part of Cedar had been trying to share the discovery of how wonderful life truly is when you drop your sword of bitterness and take responsibility for your own happiness. Her parents, however, were relentlessly committed to a lifetime feud over investment splitting and dusty antiques. Neither of those followed them to the Pearly Gates.

Cedar always described her childhood as growing up poor. Interesting. She wasn't lying, but rather she was identifying her definition of wealth. As a journalist, she roved the planet for a bit as a philanthropist. Her income wasn't geared to this but when she saw a child in need of shoes, or a single mother in desperate need to feed her family, Cedar's wallet and heart burst open.

She never married. Her friends yearned for her to feel a sense of roots, but it was as if Cedar was too fearful to return to a re-enactment of her childhood. She was the best auntie to literally hundreds around the world. Cedar never missed a birthday or a special occasion and did her absolute best to make friends with the concept of Christmas. She much preferred to surprise you with a gift on a random Tuesday for no reason than to lose herself in the frenzy of obligation.

On the day of her 45th birthday, a group of her nearest and dearest threw Cedar a surprise party. This was bold because Cedar always dodged the spotlight and declared gifts made her itch! Cedar was a giver in every sense of the word. Trying to convince her to accept anything took the negotiating tactics of a highly trained intelligence officer. Cedar would exhaust you rather than accept just a little taste of the kindness she shared effortlessly.

To prevent her from becoming overwhelmed, they decided to limit the gift to just one item. Several months prior, her dearest friends had commissioned a gorgeous cedar chest to be custom-made just for her. Upon its lid, her name "Cedar" was lovingly inscribed, and inside it held a treasure trove of her most cherished possessions: photographs, letters, and even printed-out texts, all presented on pretty paper alongside her favorite treats. This chest was a reflection of her heart, a hope chest filled with all the things she held most dear. Cedar was a woman who found her true wealth not in material possessions, but in the countless moments of joy and wonder that she collected like precious gems throughout her life. Her very vocabulary had adapted to reflect this perspective, as she described herself as "ridiculously wealthy"—a statement that spoke volumes about the abundance of love and memories that she carried within her soul.

The night lasted into the wee hours. Her tribe of friends were not heavy partiers. Most transitioned to ice water or tea by 10 p.m., including Cedar.

Cedar never lost sight of her profound and thoughtful appreciation for the beautiful friendships that graced her life. She felt a glow within as she recognized the immense value of these connections, the way they painted vibrant colours on the canvas of her existence. Each friend held a unique place in Cedar's story, their presence a gift she treasured dearly. From the late-night conversations that danced with laughter and vulnerability to the quiet moments of shared understanding; Cedar knew peace. With every shared memory, heartfelt exchange, and the simple comfort of their presence, Cedar felt blessed beyond measure, grateful for the threads of friendship that wove together the tapestry of her life. The woman in her mirror was just so very full of love. For Cedar, that was a lottery win of unimaginable happiness.

The next morning, Cedar's best friend Amy and her husband Greg drove over to Cedar's house to deliver the cedar chest. When Cedar didn't answer the door, they thought she must be out of her usual morning walk. Amy and Greg headed to the local diner for breakfast, returning about 90 minutes later. Still no Cedar. When Greg approached the back of the house he saw Cedar, still in bed. No, oh no, not Cedar.

When the police and ambulance arrived, it was determined that Cedar passed in her sleep. Her heart was full of love and perhaps, as they like to think of it, simply overflowed with happiness.

Every member of the gang now has their very own cedar chest. The beautiful engraving atop each chest, bearing the words "Forever Cedar," serves as a poignant reminder to seize each moment and treasure the memories that warm their hearts.

"Joy is what happens to us when we allow ourselves
to recognize how good things really are."
~ Marianne Williamson

CHAPTER FOURTEEN

ALICIA BUISST

Roaring On & Finishing Strong

When thinking of Alicia, you could go in a multitude of different directions. This woman was of enormous spirit. There is a rainbow to unravel in her honour. She was a devoted wife, aunt, sister, surrogate daughter, surrogate mom, and friend to souls of all sizes and vocations. A forensically organized delight of a human.

Alicia, an avid reader, was the woman who could never see any book put to death. She was a curator of joy, hope, and purpose. One classy gal, a fundraising ninja, a woman who would roar and roll through a half-marathon and the person that embodied Nelson Mandela's words, "It's always impossible until it's done." All of these would describe and capture part of the essence of this woman who was so awesomely in a league of her own.

Yet, amidst every story that family and friends can share, it invariably revolved around strength. Not the strength of bicep curls, but rather the remarkable resilience that Alicia exhibited in her life. She discovered her own means to flourish, to extend her wings, and to continuously evolve in the pursuit of making a meaningful impact. Alicia chose the path of personal growth and evolution, not just for herself, but in the truest sense of the word, "mankind."

Alicia's life can teach us all a few lessons about responding to the challenges of life. She authentically embodied our most precious inheritance; the ability to both give and receive profound love. Alicia's fortitude is broken down into many facets within the many chapters of the story of her life as she wrote it.

Born in Brooklyn, New York as 1965 was just days into its own life, the first man Alicia actually saw was her brother, Walter Jr. When Alicia's mom went into labour, her dad, Walter was at work, so Walter Jr. loaded mom into the car and drove her safely to Greenpoint Hospital in time to welcome our little firecracker into the world. This wasn't the only time Walter Jr. would contribute to his little sister's life.

Suzanne, Alicia's sister, was elated. At 8 years old, Suzanne immersed herself in the big sister role and attributes the "happy baby" sweet character of Alicia as the reason why she grew to like babies. Growing up, Suzanne witnessed her little sister stepping into a role of remarkable confidence at an early age with an intellect that was locked and loaded. Alicia was hardwired for greatness. She must have sensed it herself, as one of her favourite stops when she was out with Suzanne was always the office supply store.

As the years went by, Alicia and Suzanne would bounce ideas off each other, but Suzanne, often times, stood back and marvelled at the way her little sister would face unbelievable obstacles head-on with class and poise. When Suzanne gave birth to a beautiful daughter named Rianne, it was then Alicia's turn to become a surrogate mom. Rianne and Alicia were two peas in a pod, and just as close as if they actually lived in a pod. When Rianne was young, Alicia would watch over her and try to instill values, discipline, and a peculiar love of ceramic pigs on Rianne.

One of her strategies was to have Rianne do her pedicures and scrub her toilets. Not surprising and very congruent with her remarkable self, when Rianne grew up, Alicia returned to do her pedicures and scrub her toilets. When Rianne had her daughter Alice, Alicia was over the moon in love with her. She loved children, mentored so many of them, but Rianne and Alice... well, they were her girls.

A graduate of the University of Southern Florida, Alicia, or "Lee" as many knew her, was already soaring with her linguistic prowess. In the early 1980's she was working as the manager of the box office at the Ruth E Eckerd Hall, a Performing Arts Center in Clearwater, Florida. She never missed a beat and was the envy of many who wanted to meet the same famous people with whom she was rubbing shoulders.

By 1987, Alicia was sailing through her 20s when the deep brown eyes and engaging smile of Andy proved to be the double rainbow miracle of her life. It was like, "Oh, there you are, wowza, game over." She was enamoured with all things British before, and this just proved her love was in the right direction as Andy's cute British accent was knee-weakening with every syllable.

A proposal in the spring of 1988 on Clearwater Beach, led to an Oct. 20, 1990 wedding, followed by a hop in the car for a road-trip adventure around the southeast of the US.

In Andy's words, Alicia added a "3rd dimension to his 2-dimensional life." They are exactly 9 months apart. Andy was born brilliant and put in his order for Alicia the second she was born, only to cross the Atlantic when her soul called out to him that she was ready.

These two, as everyone knew, were two souls waiting to unite. Not only for the obvious great love they shared, but it was actually Andy that was the catalyst for the magical talents of Alicia's baking.

Recognizing her love and desire to learn, Andy knocked on the door of a baking school and signed Alicia up for classes. The next four years provided Alicia the opportunity to manifest talents akin to being a wizard of scones, pastries, cakes and even rhubarb apple crumble for Andy G., her Andy's lifelong friend, despite him crashing her motorcycle when she was away. During this chapter of her life, when she wasn't baking, she could be found tending to her cherished lilies in the garden. In fact, the flower was so special to her that she was nicknamed "Lily" after it. Alicia adored Stargazer lilies the most.

In 1994, Andy and Alicia relocated to Michigan. Neither one of them knew what the next chapters of their stories were going to entail, yet Alicia was already fully embraced in her "All things are possible" j'oie de vivre. In 1995, Alicia started her career as administrative assistant in commercial banking at Society Bank, now Key Bank in Ann Arbor, Michigan. Two young ladies, Linda and Susan, who were in charge of underwriting commercial loans, had to go through Alicia to get to the lender. Alicia was the girl that baked! Alicia was the girl that brought in cakes, chocolate chip pumpkin muffins, and rustic apple pies! Work became a literal slice of heaven. In 1996, Linda got engaged, and Alicia blew everyone away with a two-tier chocolate and vanilla cake that shone just like Alicia. When she wasn't baking for her co-workers, she was posting 3M sticky notes everywhere. Everyone stayed on task when Alicia was in the mix!

Alicia's attention to detail will be forever unrivaled and she soon became a closing specialist, putting together multi-million dollar deals. She commanded respect, and yet, simultaneously, she delivered boundless love and compassion. Alicia, Susan and Linda soon became the Power Women Trio. "Little Patty," as she was affectionately known around the office, was also blessed by Alicia. With no family of her own, and very little resources, Alicia adopted her as her surrogate Michigan mother. She filled Patty's cupboards and heart with everything she's never had but always deserved.

Patty was just one more person added to the list whose life was richer because Alicia was in it. In 1995, Alicia joined the Dale Carnegie Institute and quickly became a trainer. Little did she know, she was training herself to change the world.

Andy and Alicia were passionate world explorers! While Alicia had a deep love for England and everything related to teapots, it was Rome that truly ignited her soul. Amidst their travels in Milan, Andy was occupied with work, while Alicia and another woman indulged in the ultimate luxury—a chauffeured tour for two whole days which included the astounding World's Fair in Milan.

Andy G. would continue to travel with Andy for either pleasure or their work at PPG. Alicia's lightning-quick wit never failed as she teased the two British Andys about their "Bromance." Once, when Andy G. first came to visit them in their apartment in Michigan, he wore his hair slicked back. Alicia couldn't resist leaving a can of Crisco in the bathroom for him to find in the morning!

Whenever friends Francine and her husband, Michael, were

around, it was guaranteed to be a riot of laughter and fun! Alicia's infectious spirit was like a comedy show, leaving everyone in fits of giggles and belly laughs. Her mischievous sense of humour shone through, especially when she set her sights on her sweetheart Andy. With every teasing jab, she had everyone doubled over with laughter, and even Andy couldn't resist cracking a smile. It was always a good time with this lively group, and Alicia's playful antics were a highlight of every outing.

Everyone loved to see Andy and Alicia together. Even if Andy was working on his motorcycle in the garage and Alicia would pop in to make sure he wasn't in his "time standing still mode" as she delivered his marching orders. Andy never lost sight of two things, that, yes, "God did give you Lee" and "Yes, dear" was always an appropriate response.

Alicia was love through and through. Whether it was making friends laugh, mentoring young women in Detroit schools to gain confidence, or hosting an ice cream social, she made everyone feel like they were precious, important and limitless.

In Alicia's sphere you became an extension of her vibrancy where nothing was impossible. She lived Zig Ziglar's philosophy of "if you can dream it, you can achieve it." Make eye contact with her and she looked into your deepest recesses and helped you to light your own fire. Alicia harvested your sparkles and returned them to you so you could see just how marvelous you really are.

Then came 2007. Our energizer bunny was feeling tired. Her batteries didn't wear down easily, so it was time to see what was up. A diagnosis of blood cancer was rendered, and Alicia faced off with it.

She didn't just rise to the occasion; she broke it down, chewed it up and turned it into medicine for anyone who needed it. After all, "There's always time for a miracle." Alicia squared off with her diagnosis and went full tilt into "mission mode"—a term she coined to mean "kick ass."

Walter, her brother, was a perfect match for stems cells, and he gave willingly and prayed fiercely. Andy prayed, too. His words were, "Take me instead." Alicia enlisted her first rule of survival, which was to survive.

Alicia redefined the very essence of the word "survival" with her unyielding passion and determination. It started with walking half-marathons, then running, then running full marathons, then triathlons. In January of 2010, she saw her soon to be hero, Brad, speaking at a kick off session for Team in Training of the Lymphoma Leukemia Society. Alicia was recovering from a bone marrow transplant and was very enamoured with Brad's medals from the Disney Marathons. She looked at them and said, "I'm gonna get me those." The teams called the medals "bling" and Alicia was committed to seeing some bling around her neck.

Another forever friendship was born. The Mission IS Possible group was humming. The St. Anthony triathlon in St. Pete's, Florida required training in the pool, Kensington Park runs, spin classes, along with purple/white and green team colour finishes. There were selfies. There were sisterhoods. Endurance failures were eclipsed by Alicia's bright sparkly blue eyes.

After Alicia's first half-marathon where she walked 13.1 miles in 3 hours, 22 minutes and 25 seconds, raising $7,595 for LLS she said, "I thought about all the struggles that every one of us goes through and how our challenges and our ability to survive each day connects us. As I walked and listened to my music, I kept going and kept going and kept going. Experiences are life changing, yes, but more so they are life directing. It's about giving the best of ourselves to every day we have."

In her dear friend Janice's words, "Alicia had always been words in action, with a sense of class and grace beyond compare."

Alicia held to her word; she would relentlessly "roar" through her challenges. She was indeed fearless.

Within her six years of total remission and throughout her darkest days of relapse and treatment, she was a warrior demanding a cure; yet still, she remained a loyal friend, a sister to so many, never forgetting to ask "And how are you?"

Failure was not in her vocabulary. Alicia was a "one and done" vigilante. As we continue to tell the story of this legendary woman, it will not be about her dark hours of diagnoses, relapses, pain, or suffering. It will be her heroism and the gift of her legacy, so rich in lessons, that will remain imbedded in our hearts and shared in conversations as we go forward to conquer Alicia's highest mountain.

Words of transplants will hover around hope. Gratitude will be paid forward in honour of Alicia's family and family of friends who emptied their existence to save Alicia's. Grace will be cocooned around every soul weary in their travels.

Devotion has been redefined by virtue of the greatest love story illuminated by Andy and Alicia.

On Feb. 19, 2019 with Ann-Margaret, Alicia's dear friend, holding one hand and Andy holding the other, Alicia took her final kind breaths and became the planet's angel to help guide us to find our highest selves, while she is likely busy reorganizing the stars.

> *"We are tender and fierce, We are soft and strong. We are fragile and courageous. Sometimes all In one day."*
> *~ Unknown*

CHAPTER FIFTEEN

COLIN HARPER

Always Ready!

Colin was a man of eclectic talent. There was Colin the pilot. After earning his pilot's license in the late 1970's, he and a Cessna had many dates as he channelled his inner Chuck Yeager, within reason, of course. When his feet were on the ground Colin was the dad. In this role, he never missed a beat updating the "chore board" at home. His daughters, Debra, Lori, and Lisa, earned $0.25 for hand-clipping the hedges. Mileage on the car was logged and billed to the respective driver, but there was always the risk of a subtraction in funds as well, such as a burp erupting from Lori, standing proud in her middle child rebellion!

Colin made his debut into this world on Oct. 4, 1936, in Toronto, Ontario. While he was a steadfast Maple Leafs fan, he also dabbled in ice skating as a pastime when he was a teenager.

One day, as he was skating with his brother Bill, he spotted Jean, a cute girl who was circling the ice with her girlfriend Carol. Unfortunately, they were a little late on their potential love connection discovery as closing time came with the arena lights powering down. All hope was not lost, however, as Cupid was getting a second chance. With serendipity on their side, Colin and cutie pie Jean would be headed to the same high school the following year.

In the meantime, summer was upon them, and Colin, being the athlete that he was, also pitched for a baseball team. This enticed the not-so-sporty Jean to join a team despite having never played. The moment of truth came when she was up to bat, likely wondering what on earth she was thinking, but then remembered once her knees weakened as she glanced at Colin on the pitcher's mound. Colin wound up and sent a ball sailing over home plate, challenging Jean to swing. Jean closed her eyes, swinging with everything she had. With embarrassment averted, Jean luckily connected. The ball sputtered in a lazy roll, only to lose complete steam a couple of feet in front of Colin.

Remarkably, his finesse and coordination just happened to fail him as it never had before, allowing Jean to run all the bases and cross home plate. In the baseball world this was called a home run. In the case of Colin and Jean, it was called the beginning of forever.

It was 1952, and the young love birds dated all throughout high school. Jean described him as one of the two most handsome guys in their school. The other one was blonde. Colin was a handsome, very dark brunette, with piercing blue eyes. And he was a flirt, so this meant she had competition. But even the girl who had tried to seduce him by sharing her orange popsicle proved to be no match for the kismet shared between Colin and Jean.

Colin was the fella of continual proposals, until finally, at Christmas in 1956, he proposed at Aunt Milly's and the two, just entering their 20's, were wed on June 8, 1957. Some might have said they were too young, but after 62 years of marriage, they may recall they were right on time.

By 1968, Colin and Jean had three incredible daughters, ages 8, 7 and 3. He had left LaFrance Fire Engine and was working at Chrysler when he received a transfer notice to Windsor, Ontario. A beautiful house on Bruce Avenue in southern Ontario became their home. It was complete with stunning old hardwood floors needing polishing. Those floors soon became Debra, Lori and Lisa's nemesis and pain in the knees! It was as if Colin could smell a smudge, scratch or piece of lint invading its shine. The girls found themselves in charge of keeping the hardwood healthy with elbow grease and a few mumbles under their breath.

Colin led with an ambitious and efficient heart. We often use the term "buttoned up" to reflect being well-prepared. Colin was buttoned, bolted and zipped. This was a man that would have a 7-day shirt cycle with co-ordinating ties hung behind each shirt, ready for the work week.

Colin managed to not only give out Halloween candy in his Hulk Hogan suit, he simultaneously recorded the number of goblins that visited the porch. Colin was a man of action, conviction, and responsibility. He fulfilled his duties, even if it meant supporting others in meeting theirs.

He never complained about being the ongoing chauffeur for the girls, regardless of the time. If a co-worker had trouble climbing the stairs, Colin would carry them to their desk to ensure they could efficiently start their day.

Colin embraced the aerobics craze with zeal. Up until he was in his mid 70's, he was heading to the gym six days a week, decked out in spandex, setting up not only his, but all of his lucky lady friends' aerobic steps and equipment. GoodLife Fitness was the home of his harem. If he wasn't busy doing a grapevine, he could swing a tennis racket with amazing skill.

While Colin was a man of astounding constitution, he was also remarkably pliable at times. In 2012, the three sisters, Debra, Lori and Lisa headed down to Siesta Keys, Captiva Beach to enjoy their Christmas present from their parents. When Colin heard that they had managed to tack on two extra days to their trip, he was pleased to guard everyone's margarita sunglasses while sleeping in the car. He thought that by being absent, there were be enough beds for everyone. Thankfully the family managed to make it work and Colin happily tucked himself into his own bed those nights.

In his 82 years of living a brilliant life with a sophisticated flare for organization, Colin was an undiscovered trivia champion. Ask him anything! What was the cost of a loaf of bread in 1962? Colin could tell you. What is the best thing about birthdays? For Colin it was to sing his family anthem, "The Happy Harper Birthday Song."

Colin was a dazzler of a human being. To see him, you just have to take a look in the eyes of his wife, daughters, grandchildren and great grandchildren who still want nothing to do with those darn hardwood floors!

> *"She did not stand alone, but what stood behind her, the most potent moral force in her life, was the love of her father."*
> *~Harper Lee*

CHAPTER SIXTEEN

CONNOR O'MALLEY

Last Day Regrets

Connor was a force to be reckoned with, sassy and self-serving, as a child born and raised in the heart of Brooklyn, New York. As the youngest of seven siblings, he had inherited a legacy of Irish fire and tenacity that he was determined to uphold. At the tender age of 17, he boldly lied about his age and enlisted in the Marine Corps, following in the footsteps of his father and brothers before him. Connor was intent on forging his own path, while claiming to uphold the virtue of his family's proud military history.

However, his sister Kelly was not one to be easily swayed by Connor's "legend in his own mind" bravado, and with each exhale of her cigarette, she cut through his facade with her sharp wit and unwavering honesty.

Connor was a powerhouse, not just in brawn but in intellect beyond measure. He was the kind of young man who could bust out 100 sit-ups without breaking a sweat, then recite a Robert Frost poem with tears streaming down his face. That was just who he was—driven, passionate, and full of life.

However, when he went off to fight for his country, he failed to recognize that the real enemy was within himself. The demons inside grew fangs whenever whiskey entered his system, and he would spin delusional tales of heroism, delivered with the dramatic flair of an Emmy-winning actor. But in the end, these were just illusions, and the only person he was truly battling was himself.

In truth, Connor reported to a desk each day. The only weapon he was trained to use was a pen. Connor, a gifted linguistic, could cut with his words.

Connor's life was defined by his need for recognition and validation, driven by ideation. Despite never having seen active combat, he insinuated that he suffered from a "soul-sucking level of PTSD," which he attributed to years as a sharpshooter, taking more lives than he could ever fathom. His social media was filled with misleading quotes, and the words "Thank you for your service" only fueled his delusions, eventually leading him to believe his own lies for over 50 years.

Without a medal, uniform, or any reasonable proof of his supposed heroics, Connor created a false identity, camouflaging his psyche to bask in the adoration of his children and others.

Unaware of his deep-seated issues, his four children and three grandchildren were proud of their "hero" Patriarch. It was a tragic situation, but one that could only be resolved by confronting the truth head-on.

When backed into a corner, Connor would resort to using his faux-military trauma tales as a manipulation tactic. But if that failed, he would go even further, weaving a convoluted and deadly cancer diagnosis into his tales to weaken the hearts of those around him and make it harder for them to question his motives.

His life was a constant downward spiral as he clung to the belief that his charisma and lies would ultimately prevail. But in reality, Connor's actions only served to further damage those around him, and he was only delaying the inevitable—the truth would eventually come to light, and his lies would be exposed.

As it always does, the truth ultimately surfaced, and after claiming cancer for so many years, Connor manifested it in his body. Stage 4 liver cancer, with metastases throughout Connor's body, was swiftly invading his every cell, ultimately leaving him weak and helpless. The news was devastating, and his family was beside themselves with grief and anger.

For so long, they had lived with the burden of Connor's lies and deception. And now, as they faced the reality of his imminent death, they knew that they could not support his fraud on this sacred day. They could not, in good conscience, allow him to be honoured as a hero when he had never truly served.

It was a difficult decision, one that weighed heavily on their hearts. But in the end, they knew that it was the right thing to do. A proper military funeral was reserved for those who had served with honour and distinction, and Connor was not among them. They would honour his life in their own way, but they could not allow his lies to be perpetuated any longer.

Each family member had their own version of his stories, but none of them could quite piece together the truth. As Connor's health declined, he finally admitted to them that his life had been a lie, leaving his children feeling as though they had been living in a world of deception. They struggled to come to terms with the fact that they had told his stories with pride, only to realize that they had been perpetuating falsehoods.

The revelation that Connor had been living a lie about his identity for most of his life inflicted a profound pain upon his family. They had loved him deeply, embracing him for who he truly was, or so they believed. Trying to grapple with the truth felt like navigating a treacherous emotional landscape. Confusion, disbelief, and a profound sense of betrayal washed over them, intertwining with the love they still held for Connor. They yearned to understand the reasons behind his actions, seeking solace in memories of the person they thought they knew. In their hearts, they held onto the hope that one day, they would find a way to reconcile the truths of Connor's identity with the love they had for him, weaving together a new narrative of acceptance and forgiveness.

Connor's funeral lacked the pomp and circumstance that many had expected, leaving his children feeling a sense of panic as they struggled to explain why their father was not being honoured as a military hero. They faced questions from decorated veterans who had come to pay their respects, but were left with nothing to say.

In the end, the family realized that truth was the only thing that mattered. They loved Connor unconditionally, but had to say goodbye to him with the realization that they never really knew him.

Their message to others is that honesty is always the best policy, and that pretending to be something you're not will only lead to pain and disappointment for those who love you.

"Tell the truth, tell the truth, tell the truth."
- Sheryl Louise Moller

CHAPTER SEVENTEEN

DEMERISE VASELENIUCK

Together Again

As we think back on Demi's life, we are transported to a time when elegance and poise were the hallmarks of a true woman. She was a leader, a force to be reckoned with, who demanded first place in everything she did—even in the way she entered this world. Demi was born on Jan. 1, 1940, the first day of a new decade. It was as if she knew she was destined for greatness.

Demi's childhood in Tracadie, New Brunswick, was defined by her unique name, Demerise, which was later shortened to Demi. However, her name was just one aspect of her remarkable qualities. Over time, it became clear that the star power possessed by the many famous Demis who followed was congruent with that of our original 1940s version.

Demi's career at the Governor's Mansion in New Brunswick was nothing short of impressive, yet her heart belonged to teaching ballroom dance. Her mastery of the Latin dances was awe-inspiring, and there was an ethereal quality to her movements on the dance floor that captivated onlookers. Her teaching style was just as enchanting, as she had a gift for making her students look and feel their best. It's worth noting that Demi's striking appearance and innate elegance also landed her a side gig as a lingerie model, and it seemed that grace and poise were simply second nature to her. This born diva was entirely unfamiliar with the concepts of clumsiness or frumpiness!

During her marriage, Demi was blessed with three beautiful children, Neil, Tina and Roy. When they settled in Woodslee, Ontario for a while, the family lived in the hotel that her husband's parents owned. Soon, they got into their groove on Greenview Crescent in Windsor, Ontario, where there were a few obvious rules and regulations being established. The first one was that Mom was not a morning person! And if you got on her nerves, be prepared to run, because she was coming after you with the dreaded paint stick. And yet, Demi loved everyone who showed up after 12 noon!

Demi knew how to savour the finer things in life, especially when it came to the delectable seafood from her hometown's Atlantic waters. Capone's Restaurant was another favourite indulgence, where she would often be found dining with her son Neil and her closest comrades, Barb and Linda. While she was notoriously difficult to catch in the early hours of the day, there was one notable exception; a young and charming doctor who possessed both striking good looks and an exceptional bedside manner. When Demi's health faced a challenge, she was happy for those house calls!

As a true matriarch, Demi personified sophistication and elegance, with impeccable standards of class and beauty. Her every step exuded a Sophia Loren flair. She lived by her bible, an etiquette book, ensuring that every detail, from the table setting to the floral arrangements, was flawless. Her love for fashion extended to footwear, owning even stiletto slippers. Despite her petite 5'2" frame, she left a big impression wherever she went, embodying the essence of a superstar with each stride.

Demi even rocked a leather mini-skirt well into her 60s. She loved all things Elvis, adored white & turquoise blends, and catching an episode of Dancing with The Stars. In her mind, she was twirling about in her own suede soled shoes, pouring a glass of Neil's wine from her frosted and curved Chateau Neuf de Pape bottle, savouring every sip. Demi was a sultry, sophisticated woman who knew how to turn heads.

The passing of Demi at the age of 79 was a profound loss for everyone who knew her. It was as though they had lost a rare and precious gem that illuminated lives by virtue of her unique pizzazz. Even though science and medicine suggested cancer was the heavyweight of the match, love fueled hope of an underdog win.

Yet, as time passed, we began to understand that Demi's journey was part of a higher plan. She was not just an angel, but a being of incredible depth and grace, and her wings were needed to carry her to a greater calling.

Olivia was the apple of her grandmother Demi's eye. Demi would light up with pride while talking about Olivia's exceptional humanitarian achievements and her wise-beyond-her-years attitude of selflessness and devotion to humanity. Unfortunately, a tragic accident cut Olivia's life short only two years after Demi's passing. The loss was a heavy blow to all who knew and loved her, as her 22 years on earth were far too brief. Olivia radiated a magic that would calm the waters of turmoil before they could even gain momentum.

With every rainbow that now appears, we are reminded that Demi and Olivia are using their boundless energy and passion to gently awaken the world. They prompt us to choose faith over fear, and to approach life with compassion and empathy. Their presence is felt in the soft little reminders that they send us, nudging us to be the one who cares, to extend kindness and understanding to those around us. To dance! Their legacy is one of love and light, inspiring us to be better and to do better every day.

Their family, once enveloped in grief, now stands united in their mission to honour Demi and Olivia's memory. They channel their pain into purpose, advocating for greater understanding and acceptance. Through their efforts, they seek to create a world where every person can embrace their true selves without worry or judgment. With unwavering determination, they are committed to turning their heartbreak into a catalyst for change, igniting a ripple effect of love and leadership that extends far beyond their own lives. In their courageous pursuit, they carry the spirits of Demi and Olivia, ensuring that their legacy of love, vibrancy and signature sweetness will forever illuminate the lives of those they touch.

"Let no one ever come to you without leaving better and happier.
Be the living expression of God's kindness: kindness in your face,
kindness in your eyes, kindness in your smile."
- Mother Teresa

CHAPTER EIGHTEEN

DOUG ANGLIN

$2.00 Budget Bliss

From the shores of Wales to the bustling city of Montreal, Doug's journey began on Jan. 1, 1926. At just four years old, he and his family embarked on a life-changing voyage aboard the TSS Laurentic, arriving in Canada on April 27, 1930. Little did they know that their timing was impeccable, as the very ship that brought them to their new home was later destroyed by the Germans during WWII.

While Montreal became their initial home, Doug's journey led him and his family to a charming residence on Lauzon Road in Windsor, Ontario during his teenage years. And it was here, in this quaint abode, that Doug's life took a turn towards something truly magical. For he was about to embark on a love story that would become the stuff of legends: a tale of passion, commitment, and unwavering devotion that would inspire generations to come.

In the neighborhood, there was a young girl who was the epitome of beauty, grace, and spirit. Kay was a jaw-dropping knockout who left everyone spellbound with her presence. And if there is such a thing as soulmates, then Doug and Kay were it.

Doug presented Kay with a $10 engagement ring that radiated with love and elegance. It was a treasure she proudly showed off, especially when success and abundance blessed them. Their relationship was rooted in the sweet spot of unconditional love, mutual respect, easy-going laughter, and tender moments of the most beautiful friendship.

On June 5, 1947 (even though there was a typo on their marriage certificate that said 1948), Doug and Kay vowed to spend their lives together. They would love, respect, forgive, cherish, laugh, travel, and even gnaw their way through Kay's most overcooked porkchops!

And even when Doug's infamous question, "Jesus Christ, what the hell is wrong with you?" popped up, everyone knew that this was Doug's brave attempt at being angry. If you looked closely his grin was reaching up under his giggling eyes.

Doug and Kay had found the holy grail of balance. While Doug was busy building his business with his father, Riverside Welders, creating everything from clothesline poles to porch railings, Kay was the heart of their home, the glue that held everything together. With three children—Robert, Dennis and Darlene—the family was thriving.

But Doug's entrepreneurial spirit wouldn't let him rest. At just 29 years old, he opened Riverside Fabrication in 1955, moving the business to Matthew Brady Blvd. He was determined to grow the company, but he also knew the importance of having fun.

Every Saturday night, he and Kay would take $2.00 out of his paycheck and hit the town in style. They'd indulge in 10 cent draft beers, preferably Blue Light, at the Tecumseh house, before possibly heading to the Pomegranate Restaurant.

Their greatest joy, however, was found in camping. They'd venture to the French River, or a Peterborough cottage, or even in the trailer Doug built with his father, George. It didn't matter where or how they camped, as long as they were together. For them, that was where true wealth was found. And if you asked Doug, a Burnt Almond Chocolate bar was the cherry on top of a great day.

Through all their adventures and business ventures, Kay remained the best mom ever to their children, always holding down the fort and being the rock of their family. Together, they had found the perfect balance between work and play, family and fun.

Doug was a true gem, always radiating joy and amusement. His wisdom was unparalleled, and his advice was both practical and humorous. One of his most unforgettable tips was, "If you're planning to drive home tonight, don't forget to bring a car." Total Dad joke! His quick wit and lighthearted personality brought laughter and happiness to everyone around him.

Doug and Kay were not ones to let a diagnosis slow them down. When Doug was diagnosed with macular degeneration at the age of 50, Kay became his trusted co-adventurer, chauffeuring him around like a Miss Daisy. They set out to explore the world together, from Cancun to Nashville, where they danced the night away at Tootsies. Their hearts were also truly captured by Bradenton, Florida. For forty years, they journeyed to their sanctuary condo, relishing the warm sun and embracing life to the fullest.

Doug may have been retired, but he was far from idle. He happily joined the band at Leyland County Jamborees, while Kay tried her best to keep him in line. Doug even earned the honourary title of "Mayor of Windsor" in that condo community, reveling in the silliness and adoring the fun he was having alongside his best girl Kay. Their playful banter continued even over the phone, with Doug cheekily asking callers if they were sober, when it might have just been the pot calling the kettle black.

Doug carved his own path and left nuggets of laughter everywhere he went. He may have forgotten to shift his boat out of gear when friends came to visit the Ford canal, and he might have preferred dimmer lighting in his house of many windows, but he had a fantastic taste in hockey teams, being a devoted fan of the Montreal Canadiens. And until his very last moments, he couldn't resist complimenting his Kay, the core of his world and the light of his heart, on how stunning she looked in her 20-year-old sweater.

Every ounce of Doug's being appreciated the life he was blessed to build and enjoy. However, on March 1, 2019, he was admitted to the hospital due to high blood pressure and other health complications. After undergoing several procedures, Doug had had enough and expressed his desire to leave the hospital. Specifically, he said, "Get me the hell out of here!"

It was clear that his higher self was guiding him, and he knew that he needed to be in the place where he belonged—with his beloved wife, Kay.

Doug was leaving this world, and he wanted to do it in the arms of the woman he had spent 72 years with. He made sure to look Kay in the eyes and reflect on their wonderful life together. He took this opportunity, the gift where time was so delicate and precious, to acknowledge all of the love and gentle life-giving blessings that he had enjoyed on his journey.

In his final moments, Doug desired to gift Kay with the memory of their life together, and he accomplished just that. He wrapped all of the love he had left in his body around her before his left this world. On April 8, 2019, at 93 years young and surrounded by immeasurable love, Doug peacefully accepted his wings while sitting in his favourite chair with Kay by his side.

As his spirit took flight, a profound stillness filled the room, intermingled with a bittersweet serenity. Though the pain of loss lingered, Kay clung to the precious memories they had shared throughout their journey. In her heart, she carried the laughter, the embraces, and the whispered words of love that had woven their lives together. Doug's presence would be forever felt, guiding her forward with an unwavering warmth and a reminder that true love transcends the boundaries of life and death.

> *"Every heart sings a song, incomplete, until another heart whispers back. Those who wish to sing always find a song. At the touch of a lover, everyone becomes a poet."*
> *~ Plato*

CHAPTER NINETEEN

DANIELLA DEMERS

Never Miss the Chance

Her twins, Danielle and Daniel, were born to Mom Daniella when she was 16. Everyone always laughed at their names, but Mom said she chose them to keep them close. It worked. Daniella went from honour roll and varsity team captain, to a young woman with two kids shunned by judgement at every turn. The photos of her the year her babies were born reveal a beauty that was beyond stunning. She was judged for that, too. With so many obstacles in front of her, her family urged first, then demanded second, that she put her babies up for adoption. The father had already vanished into thin air. Daniella was already a mother is every sense of the word. Her babies were her treasures and she vowed to fiercely protect them.

"The moment a child is born, the mother is also born. She never existed before. The woman existed, but the mother, never. A mother is something absolutely new." - Osho

Next came hairdressing school, made possible by other teenage friends willing to babysit. From there, she opened up shop and became a true artist of her craft. Her kids thrived, yet were acutely aware of Mom's life of sacrifice. Danielle was always asked who her older sister was, and Daniel was teased about his "hot Mom". And yet, their Mom was just that, she was just Mom.

She put her children through university without either one of them owing even a dime of debt. She made holidays magical, and bad times better times. She did it with grace, humility, and poise. Most of all, she did it alone. No one knew why. There were plenty of suitors begging for a chance, but she just couldn't open herself up to that. Her words were that both sides of her heart were already taken. Many realize that she had no idea how to be taken care of and was afraid to try.

On a chilly Saturday, Daniella called her son to apologize that she would be about an hour late to pick up her grandchildren as promised. She just wasn't feeling great. Daniel gave it 15 minutes, called Daniella, then went to his Mom's. "She's just 52, eats well, exercises all the time and looks like a million bucks," but the worry consumed them. Instincts, they are never wrong, especially when you so want them to be. Doctors say her heart of gold ceased suddenly, likely minutes after she hung up the phone. Their last words were, as always, "I love you."

Never miss the chance to say, "I love you."

"I want my children to have all the things I couldn't afford.
Then, I want to move in with them."
~Phyllis Diller

CHAPTER TWENTY

JIM RUSTON

Proudest Girl Dad

I magine this: a scene that defies all logical explanation, a moment that will leave you in shock and disbelief. As I stood there, my eyes widened in awe and my jaw dropped in utter astonishment. I couldn't believe what I was witnessing.

Suddenly, out of nowhere, Jim made an abrupt and incredibly unexpected leap, ultimately rolling himself out of reach under the table. Yes, you read that right. Jim had just defied the laws of physics and made a daring escape.

I looked around and saw that I wasn't the only one in disbelief. Everyone in the room had eyes as big as saucers and jaws dangling in astonishment. Nobody would have ever expected this behavior out of him. I mean, how could they? Jim was in an urn, for crying out loud! Even Peter, the always smiling Funeral Director seemed to break out in a bit of a sweat.

Get ready to embark on a journey through the fascinating life of Jim, a man whose story will inspire and move you. It all started on a picturesque autumn day, Sept. 30, 1944, when the world welcomed him into existence. The air was crisp, the leaves were turning gold, and the number one song on the charts was Bing Crosby's "Swinging on a Star." Little did we know that this would be the perfect theme for Jim's life, as he would go on to swing from his own star.

Jim was a born athlete, a natural talent on both the baseball diamond and hockey rink. He was a great sport, always pushing himself to be better, except for the occasional tantrum when he let in a sloppy goal. He was a true champion, and when he graduated from St. Rose High School, he took the title of Top Athlete with him to General Amherst High School for grade 13.

It was there, in grade 13, that Jim experienced a phenomenal encounter with Cupid. Thirteen seemed to be his lucky number, as he met Lydia, the love of his life, a sweet young girl with a vibrant smile. It was all thanks to Jim's sister Elaine, who had the keen sense to introduce the two on a Friday the 13th in September of 1963. From that moment on, their love story was one that most would buy the movie rights to experience.

With a heart full of love and a thirst for more, that same year, Jim left his job at Marvin Bondy's gas station and answered the call to create a bigger life for himself. He knew he had made the right choice as soon as he began his career at Chrysler.

Quickly climbing the ladder, he found himself in management, driven by an unwavering commitment to his work and the life he had built with his loved ones. No obstacle could stand in his way, not when he had so much love and joy waiting for him at home.

In the whirlwind of life's hustle and bustle, two years flew by for Jim and Lydia. But through it all, Jim held onto the love that brought them together, never forgetting the spark that ignited their romance. Jim proposed to Lydia at the Elmwood Casino on Nov. 10, 1965, with the sweet melody of "Put Your Head On My Shoulder" by Paul Anka in the background. Then, on May 21, 1966, they exchanged vows at St. John's Church, sealing their love and setting off on a journey that would be full of love, family, and adventure.

By 1970, with three daughters under the age of two, Jim and Lydia embraced the adventure of parenthood with open arms. They always put their family first, creating unforgettable memories and experiences along the way. Their daughters, Michelle, Debbie and Denise learned the value of simplicity and creativity, blending potato chips with sand in their playpen at White Sands Beach. There was no prouder "Girl Dad" on the planet!

Jim and Lydia were a couple that shared magical tricks stored up their sleeves. They turned baseball tournaments into monumental family vacations, and transformed their family boat, "Sunnyside," into a beloved member of the family, providing much-needed relief and respite during hot summer days. Their unwavering commitment to each other and their family created a life filled with endless possibilities and unforgettable moments that would last a lifetime. And through it all, Jim never missed a day of work. For he knew that his commitment to his family and his job were equally important.

Jim was a man whose heart was larger than life itself. His love for those around him was his shining attribute, and he showed it in every way possible. Even after retirement, Jim and Lydia continued to embrace life and all its adventures, always coaxing their family to come along. Trips to Florida and Arizona were never complete without their tribe by their side. Even Lake Havasu had the pleasure of hosting the inseparable lovebirds and their impeccable family.

As Jim approached his 75th spin around the sun, foreboding clouds started looming around his health. Despite the best efforts of doctors to figure out the root cause, they could only treat his symptoms. Worry and wonder went into overtime, yet Jim's gentle nature and magnetic personality were impossible to resist. Every nurse who had the privilege of caring for him was immediately captivated. They affectionately referred to him as "Popsy," a testament to the endearing impression he left on them all.

In what felt like the blink of an eye, eight months had passed since Jim's health had taken a turn. Within that time, it was all hands on deck at the family headquarters. Jim's daughters transformed into fire-breathing love dragons, offering their expertise, learning from each other, and pouring every ounce of care and devotion into their father, just as he had done for them throughout their lives.

As they wheeled him around, it became a bit of a sitcom. They announced themselves with a smile and a wink, "Welcome to the Promenade Deck. Please keep your hands inside." And after each performance, they were rated as Jim encouraged them to strive for excellence!

Through it all, their love for Jim burned brighter than ever before. They refused to let the situation defeat them, and instead rose to the challenge with courage, determination, and a fierce loyalty to their beloved father. It was a true testament to the power of love and the strength of family bonds.

It was just another day for Jim and his gang on March 26, 2022, as they headed out to the casino. Jim tried his luck at the slots, then relished a scrumptious dinner at his favourite restaurant, Spagos. However, it was only three days later, on March 30, when his decline began to show, and the angels arrived to rally around him.

The EMS professionals who transported Jim to the hospital were nothing short of incredible, and once there, Jim's ever-alert presence lit up the room whenever his grandkids, Alex, Ayden, Jacob, Meaghan, Justin, Adrian and Rosella spoke to him. With little warning, on April 6, Jim's condition took another downward turn, leading to increased concern and urgency amongst his medical specialists and caregivers.

Although everyone worked hard to determine the cause of Jim's decline, the answer remained a mystery, leaving the possibility open that one day, the truth would be revealed.

Amidst the excitement of Tiger Woods teeing off in the Masters on April 9, 2022, Jim transcended into his own horizon at 77 years young, surrounded by immeasurable love. His life had been a grand slam, leaving behind cherished memories and gratitude in the hearts of all who knew him.

We all wish to leave an imprint when we leave, even if it's a small gesture that brings a smile to others' faces when they think of us.

As for Jim, his final act was a testament to his inner athlete, a last little stunt that he wanted everyone to remember him by.

"Family is not an important thing. It's everything."
- Michael J. Fox

CHAPTER TWENTY - ONE

ROSA STRANO

Don't be a Karen ~ be a Rosa!

The world was turned inside out, shaken, stirred and fragmented during the pandemic. COVID-19 sunk its fangs into not just our bodies but our spirits, taking hostages in ways we never thought possible. COVID-19 took Rosa and her loved ones away from her when hands could have been held till the very last breath.

It is up to us to all do our part to right this ship of life, not just for ourselves but for the young souls that do not know what the joy of connection can bring.

We now become the soldiers and warriors in a crusade to bring the same purity of love, the same shelter of communication and concern, and the same level of extraordinary loving actions and intentions to others that Rosa did. Through this commitment to share what she embodied in her life; we have her pumping our hearts each and every day. In one word, Rosa was "together-ness."

We are all in this together, linked to bring the same goodness to the world that Rosa modelled.

Dear God,
I give this day to You.
May my mind stay centered on the things of spirit.
May I not be tempted to stray from love.
As I begin this day, I open to receive You.
Please enter where You already abide.
May my mind and heart be pure and true, and may I not deviate from the things of goodness.
May I see the love and innocence in all mankind, behind the masks we all wear and the illusions of this worldly plane.
I surrender to You my doings this day.
I ask only that they serve You and the healing of the world.
May I bring Your love and goodness with me, to give unto others wherever I go.
Make me the person You would have me be.
Direct my footsteps, and show me what You would have me do.
Make the world a safer, more beautiful place.
Bless all Your creatures.
Heal us all, and use me, dear Lord, that I might know the joy of being used by You.
~ Illuminata by Marianne Williamson

Rosa embodied every single word of that prayer since she first landed her sparkle of life on Oct. 12, 1936. She was likely as beautiful as the colours of the season. Rosa was the true middle child, being the third of six siblings, all of whom she adored with every fibre of her being. The stretch from the oldest to the youngest was 21 years, so all kinds of bonds could be woven.

Rosa was born a caregiver. As a young girl in Solano, Italy, she shared her time balancing. At one moment, she was balancing a container filled with 5 gallons of water on her head, making her way home alongside her sister Vincenza, and the next moment she was balancing her affection as she cared for her younger siblings Josie, Rocky and Mary.

Always adaptive, Rosa transitioned through their move to Argentina to settle in Windsor, Ontario, ultimately meeting her husband Mario and sharing 63 years of marriage and memories after sealing their love on July 6, 1957.

As a registered practical nurse, Rosa worked at Hotel Dieu Hospital, often taking a bit of heat for surrendering her breaks and lunches in order to provide extra care to her patients. With her daughters, Tina, Sara and Rosemarie at home, Rosa incredibly worked full time, and her kids were blissfully unaware.

Each morning, when they woke up, Rosa was there. Likely, the big breakfast of ground beef, scrambled eggs and a side of cucumbers was waiting. With full bellies, they'd be kissed and hugged as they started their days.

Dinners and snacks, also blended with equal love to ingredients, were provided before a bedtime story, likely including the little lamb in the meadow. And once her angels were sleeping, Rosa was off to the Hotel Dieu to heal and hold.

Rosa's ultimate happiness came when she became a Nonna. There was nothing more precious in her life than creating a feast on Christmas Eve, followed by a sea of presents (not so secretly) stored in her closet, carting her little darlings around in her teal Tempo, and safeguarding their sleeping selves by the protective measures of placing dining room chairs around their beds.

Rosa's life was celebrated on Oct. 10, 2022 which was also World Mental Health Day. Each one of us, as humans, have known sadness, anxiety, a state of angst where the ground just refuses to stop moving. It is simply not right that we feel we must become proficient in concealing our angst under a smile. Whatever it looks like to ourselves or to someone else, we need to increase our dosage of kindness in terms of treatment.

There were days that family walked into Rosa's house, Thursday's to be exact, when she was a cleaning fanatic. All things getting dusted or the floors scrubbed and shined, by virtue of Nonna being on her knees doing so.

Perhaps she was truly on her knees? Physically and proverbial. And how wonderful it was that her family walked in to bring some sunshine. We all need to be each other's sunshine.

Thanksgiving is my favorite holiday. This is the day where gratitude is the attitude. Standing in the midst of gratitude fills me with the greatest joy. It requires my heart to be open to love. Love that is simple, yet profound. Sometimes I chuckle to myself, thinking how "simple love" is an oxymoron, like "jumbo shrimp." Perhaps, "jumbo love" would be a more fitting term. But maybe the phrase "pure and simplistic love" describes it best. It is a type of love that effortlessly fills you with contentment and a sense of wholeness. And when you feel it land, either on beautiful little babies' feet, the colour of the autumn leaves, someone's smile, a rose or hibiscus flower, or most importantly, the place where Rosa is held in each heart she touched, it just makes sense. It brings you to a sense of wholeness. A strength to extend ourselves in loving and grateful ways.

In honour of Rosa, let's revise the mantra to be, "In a world of Karens, be a Rosa!"

"And if, when it is all over, I am asked what I did with my life,
I want to be able to say…. I offered love."
~ Terri St. Cloud

CHAPTER TWENTY - TWO

A KELLY MELOCHE MOMENT

My Flame

Yesterday, one of my favourite people on the planet asked me if I thought it would be weird if she attended an Ash Wednesday service. I knew immediately why she asked and what she was feeling. Through baptism, she is Catholic. Through life she is non-denominationally kind, accepting and sensitive.

The world had been weighing heavily on all our shoulders, and hers were aching. It was not yet 9 a.m. Little did I know how this conversation, this thick emotion, would continue showing up for the rest of the day. Different faces in different places. Every single soul weary. The illusions of our worldly plane and the masks we all wear were losing their powers. Hour by hour, it seemed.

I was oblivious. No, that's a lie. A tsunami of something was rumbling in the distance, evident in the tears of every person seated in front of me grieving the loss of a 61-year-old who had way too much charisma and fire to be taken away without warning.

By 11:30 a.m., the next level of my emotional armour was minus two more layers. I am known for deviating from my own script when I lead a Celebration of Life, but this time I felt like I was being hijacked by a greater purpose.

I saw the magic of a packed room filled with love. Different faces from different places, jobs, shapes, sizes, colours and contexts. All together. Bound by love. The light in the darkness. Fuel for our souls. I was imagining it rippling out over our wounded planet.

By 4 p.m., I was walking my dog while thinking about my daily yoga practice. I never really got yoga, but it seems yoga has got me. It's a moving metaphor: heart openers to remain receptive, grounding to stand strong in your essence while offering roots and branches to those who may need to grab hold. Drop your shoulders (worries), create space and nurture flexibility in all realms of your spiritual, physical, mental and emotional being. Be present.

I thought of how hard that was. Being present. It made me wonder if everyone found the sharp edges of rogue negativity bleeding their spirit too. Brené Brown, my very best friend that

I've never met, has this wonderful lesson that she taught her kids and one I wish I had known to teach mine.

Brené would have her kids cup their hands. She would then explain that within their hands is their flame. It is their light, their soul, their spirit. She taught them to surround themselves with friends, whom when they saw their light shining bright, would never feel the need to blow it out. And, on the days when it is windy and stormy, you want a good friend that will cup their hands around yours to protect your light.

It's now 7 p.m., and I am acutely aware of how unpleasant being "un-present" feels. I tried to do yoga. I made strange with the flavour of Zen. Even Adriene's cherub You Tube approach could not settle me. Then my phone rang. It was someone calling to cup their hands around my flame. Another kindred soul texted, randomly on time.

My hands were not cupped around my own flame. I'm not sure whether it was my sputtering light, or my hands flailing around claiming unworthiness to rise, but I am so grateful hands arrived to breathe life into my light.

All this sounds dramatic but, in truth, it was just a bad day. A bad day as described by a girl that can tell a great story. My self-diagnosis was that I had the "empath blues."

We've all had way too many bad, frustrating, empty, lonely, numbing and terrifying days. In my quest to understand the light and darkness, I chose to hurl myself into both with zero concept of what I would do with my findings. Total squirrel in the middle of the road plan of attack.

Andy is a cherished friend in my life that often asks me how "TKW" is. That means "The Kelly Within". A thoughtful question that we should all ask each other, and ourselves. If you are reading this, know my hands are cupped around your flame.

> *"So often, when we feel lost, adrift in our lives, our first instinct is to look out into the distance to find the nearest shore. But that shore, that solid ground, is within us. The anchor we are searching for is connection, and it is internal."*
> *— Brené Brown*

CHAPTER TWENTY - THREE

CONSIDER THIS

Ultimately, we are on this planet, experiencing this life, to evolve as loving beings. If you watch a baby, it lights up at a smile, a gentle touch and is always curious about life. As we grow, it is who we are that matters most, not what we have. We understand that life is far more than anything you can ever see, hear or touch. We are capable of achieving all of our dreams. We are brilliant beings, knowing beings, understanding beings always available to offer and embrace forgiveness, marvel at a sunset, find fascination in a butterfly, smile at a friendly face, strive to connect and thrive in allowing.

In every moment, we are validated in our own essence while casting our net to achieve our dreams. We have the ability to share compassion as easy as oxygen and realize that laughter really is the best medicine. And so, when we lose someone we love, we can then reconcile that we didn't lose the love, we just can't touch the form. And since we cannot physically touch fascination, happiness, passion, joy, ease, anticipation, curiosity, excitement or gratitude, yet they can overwhelm us and saturate us in their glory, we must look at death the same way. This love, the love you have for anyone that you love and have lost, is still fully alive and a wholly pervasive feeling. The person or the pet remains just as strongly in your heart, mind and vision as when they were physically here. The love is reciprocal. The gratitude eternal.

Every person has a unique story to tell, filled with experiences and memories that have shaped them into the person they are today. Each individual has a different perspective and a different journey that has led them to where they are. Regardless of background or circumstance, every life has value and every person has the potential to make a difference in the world.

It is important to recognize the significance of our stories and the impact they can have on others. By sharing our experiences, we can offer guidance, hope, and inspiration to those around us. Our stories can serve as a source of comfort and encouragement, reminding others that they are not alone in their struggles.

Through our actions and words, we have the power to write our chapters in a way that will inspire future generations. We can choose to live our lives with purpose, compassion, and kindness, leaving a positive legacy that will continue to impact the world long after we are gone. By living our lives in this way, we can encourage others to do the same and create a ripple effect of positivity and change.

"Please Don't Die with Your Gifts Inside"
~Amber Rae